Marriage Licenses

of

Caroline County, Maryland,

1774-1815

BY

HENRY DOWNES CRANOR

Reprinted from The Pennsylvania Magazine of History and Biography

PHILADELPHIA

1904

Notice

In many older books, foxing (or discoloration) occurs and, in some instances, print lightens with wear and age. Reprinted books, such as this, often duplicate these flaws, notwithstanding efforts to reduce or eliminate them. The pages of this reprint have been digitally enhanced and, where possible, the flaws eliminated in order to provide clarity of content and a pleasant reading experience.

Marriage Licenses of Caroline County, Maryland, 1774-1815

Originally published
Philadelphia
1904

Reprinted by:

Janaway Publishing, Inc.
732 Kelsey Ct.
Santa Maria, California 93454
(805) 925-1038
www.janawaygenealogy.com

2015

ISBN: 978-1-59641-344-3

MARRIAGE LICENSES OF CAROLINE COUNTY, MARYLAND, 1774-1815.

[Caroline County, Maryland, was formed in 1774 from parts of the counties of Dorchester and Queen Anne. The licenses have been copied from the records in the office of the Clerk of the Court of the county, and but one year (1776) is missing. No attempt has been made to correct the spelling of any of the names, some of which are almost undecipherable on the record. From 1774 to 1804 the license fee was one pound, and subsequently four dollars.]

1774.

April 6. John Pritchett Fisher and Ruth Thomas.
11. Solomon Brady and Margaret Bailey.
27. John Lucas and —— Morgan.
John Cooper and Eliza Lucas.
May 6. Edward Minnier and Priscilla Collison.
20. Jacob Wootters and Mary Jump.
Joshua Willis and Deborah Greehawk.
22. James Wainwright and Elizb^{th} Berry.
25. William Williams and —— Merrick, Queen Ann Co.
June 1. Thomas Orrell and Sarah Sommers.
Nathan Downes and Ann Cooper.
14. Tobias Burk and Sarah Stainer.
21. Joseph Ward and Lydia Jones.
William Banning and Rebecca Cheez.
July 7. Hebijah —— and —— Walker, of Queen Ann Co.
August 3. Solomon Wilson and Hannah Bett or Belt.
Washington Gibson, of Talbot Co., and Rebecca Brutt, of same.
MacCabee Alford and Rachel Bozman.

3

August 14. William Parrish and Rachel Harwood.
16. Richard Dudley and Mary Manship.
17. Samuel Fountain and —— Fountain.
John Culbreth and Sarah Bradley.
Capt. Samuel Nicholson and Pr. Force.
24. William Clayton and Sarah Vanderford, of Queen Ann Co.
25. Thomas Parratt Roe and Jane Clark, of Talbot Co.
29. John Price or Rice and Elizabeth Clark, of Talbot Co.
Nathan Nickerson and Mable Grace, of Caroline Co.
September 4. Park Webb and Mary Fountain, of Dorchester Co.
6. Bozman Harwood and Ann Harwood, of Dorchester Co.
8. Carter Cochran and Rebecca Clough, of Talbot Co.
10. James Snitch and Rebecca Flaharty.
14. William Chilton and Rebecca Talbot.
Gally Lane and Araminta Dial.
16. Ezekiel Smith and Ann Jacobs.
20. Jonas Jones and Eliza Sill.
28. John Frantum and Eliza Hopkins Shannahan, of Talbot Co.
29. Daniel Skinner and Mary Casson.
October 3. Robert Hopkins and Dorcas Hooper.
John Porter and Lydia Kinnannon.
16. John Gregory and Ann Armstrong.
James Gregory and Eliza Bush.
19. Daniel Hart and Sarah Lockerman.
25. James Ayres and Ann Griffin, of Talbot Co.
29. Timothy Price and Ann Dudley,   do.
31. Hezekiah Coxill and Eliza Carter.
November 5. William Price and Mary Birkham.
December 3. Moses Butler and Elonor Plumer.

Received by William Richardson, Deputy Clerk, and disposed of as follows, to wit.

December James Russmer and Ann Martindale.
12. William Batchelor and Margaret McCan.
20. John Willoughby and Ann Walker.

1775.

January 28. Levin Blades and Betsey Newman.
Daniel Polk and Margaret Miller White.
Perdue Martindale and Anna Andrew.
Curtis Jacobs and Polly Cannon.
Joseph Bradley and Betsey Richards.
Risdon Fisher and Mary Parker.
Zepheniah Polk and Lucretia Cawsey.
Joseph Frantom and Mary Ann Gamor.
Charles Duffin and —— Bozman.
John Marshall and —— Sherwood.
James Merrick and Tilpha Quarternnis.
Thomas Hancock and Cleia Morris.
William Owens and Elizabeth Meffin.
Edward Smith and Elizabeth Baxter.
John Kirby and Sarah Kirby.
Archibald Smith and Sarah McCullum.
Thomas Robinson and Sarah Tool.
Elijah Charles and Hebe Moore.

Received by William Richardson, Deputy Clerk, 24 Marriage Licenses, and disposed of in the manner following.

William McMahon and Catharine Mifflin.
James Porter and Sophia Parmarr.
August 9. Francis Claymore and Nancy Cleft.
Nicholas Goldsborough and Rebecca Myers.
Robert Lloyd Nicols and Susanna Chamberlane.
William Colescott and Mary Wheatley.
Richard Boswell and Mary Davis.
Abnor Roe and Julia Sylvester.

August   9. Robert Nutter and Sarah Bagwell.
John Stevens and Ann Anderson.
Matthew Pawson and Mary Caulk.
Joseph Daffin and Eleonar Ennals.
William Jacobs and Elizabeth Bowdle.
Richard Stanford and Hester Ann Russnur.
Parker Selby and Priscilla Fountain.
James Summers and Abisha French.
Richard Lockerman and Mary Darden.
Thomas Smith and Deborah Pratt.
John Anderson and Elizabeth Horney.
Richard Thomas and Rhoda Porter.
Richard Kennard and Anne Carroll.
James Barnulle Jr. and Sarah Charshe.
John Reynolds and Elizabeth Pennington.

October 30. To 24 Marriage Licenses received by him and disposed of, viz.
Moses Floyd and Drucilla Rumbly.
John Roberts and Mary Horney.
William Dudley and Sarah Nicols.
James Boon and Mary Toolson.
George Stevens and Sarah Bayley.
Ambrose Goslin and Elizabeth Brown.
John Cheever and Sarah Chalaghane.
Skinner Newman and Mary Bozman.
Woolman Emerson and Esther McGregory.
John O'Bryan and Sarah McGinney.
William Coplen and Elizabeth Shaw.
Robert Hardcastle and Mary Sylvester.
James Barwick and Rebecca Roberts.
Christopher Driver and Sarah Ringgold.
John Oram and Mary Marshall.,
Robert Ethernson and Rachel Santee.
James Truit and Sarah Williams.
Henry Mason and Esther Baggs.
John Tull and Catherine Merrell.
John Chelcott and Eliza Hill.

October 30. John Staut and Mary Carter.

Samuel Thomas and Margaret Oldham.

Shadrach Liden and Rebekah Fogwell.

John Keets and Ann Chalaghand.

1777.

May —. Joshua Chipley and Mary Hunter.

June 12. William Garey and Henny Garland.

27. William Martindale and Esther Baynard.

28. Jethro Virison and Mary Ann Leverton.

July 17. James Shields and —— Tarman.

18. Oliver Hackett Jr. and Ann Wilson.

21. James Fisher and Mary Holson.

23. John Plummer and Sarah Phillips.

August 9. George Downes and Ann Hall.

22. John Malcolm and Mary Lawrence.

25. James Higgins and Hannah Jarmen.

26. James Sullivane and Margaret Wheatley.

October 26. Elijah Taylor and Ann Griffith.

29. James Scott and Ann Shaw.

November 12. Jadwin Montague and Henrietta Hynson.

18. John Cohee and Celia Clark.

December 8. William Dowins and Rachel Dawson.

21. Richard Oxenham and Elizabeth Rathall.

23. William Tull and Mary Grace.

31. George Turner and —— Smith.

1778.

January 2. Thomas Hughlett and Rebekah Mason.

4. John Ireland and Ann Alford.

9. William Goult and Saphira Baynard.

10. Samuel Shelton Stop and Margaret Douglass.

14. Isaac Jump and Sarah Leverton.

16. John Mitchell and Sarah Scott.

18. William Bullin and Elizabeth Barmooll.

21. Nathan Madden and Ann Hutton.

23. Andrew Price and Prudence White.

January 26. Joseph Boone and Rebekah Cox.
     27. Nicholas Wood and Ann Clark.
     30. Robert Jones and Deborah Downes.
February 3. John Molony and Eleonar Anthony.
     4. James Fisher and Nice Turner.
    10. Thomas Roe and Mary Baggs.
    11. Jacob Jump and Mary Leverton.
    13. Littleton Berry and Mary Towers.
    15. David Craig and Ann Merchant.
    23. James Larey and Elizabeth Morgan.
    " James Slemarr and Mary Exbanks.
    24. James Harris and Katharine Dodd.
    25. James Barwick and Cordelia Hynson.
    " William Whiteley and Sarah Baynard.
March 7. Samuel Fountain and Elizabeth Purnell.
    22. Nathaniel Potter and Jane Douglass.
April 1. Solomon Barwick and Ross Lawful.
    19. John Allen and Rebeckah Smith.
    25. Robert Waddell and Elizabeth Ball.
    29. George Plowman and Elizabeth Millington.
    Christopher Jump and Hannah Wootters.
May 11. Vincent Pinkind and Rebekah Young.
    12. Richard Browning and Rebekah Camp.
    15. James Matthews and Alice Faulkner.
    20. Thomas Larrimore and Rebekah Frampton.
    Archibald Jackson and Susannah Jackson.
    30. George Bell and Elizabeth Pinkerton.
June 3. John Jones and Elizabeth Roberts.
    7. John Erichston and Hannah Hollis.
    12. John Trimbly and Rachel James.
July 6. John Payne and Elizabeth Parker.
    16. Richard Ozmont Jr. and Elizabeth La-
    compte.
    Benjamin Kelly and Leveniah Johnson.
    24. John Merrick and China Dixon.
    28. Charles Manship and Ann Bland.
    Aaron Manship and Sarah Bland.

August   6. Richard Smith and Sarah Banning.
       10. George Bright and Rachel Chapman.
       12. James Dilling and Tilley Blades.
September 1. Luke Andrew and Mary Rowins.
         James Blades and Sidney Jordan.
       9. James Hambleton and Elizabeth Dawson.
     14. Jacob Wootters and Mary Warner.
     21. Benthal Stevens and Mary Newells.
     22. Raleigh Marshall and Mary Barwick.
     26. John Sylvester and Elizabeth Fisher.
     28. William Smith and Ann Green.
     29. John Robinson and Amelia Sullivane.
October 2. Perry Garmon and Esther Andrew.
      7. Thomas Smith and Katharine Price.
     13. Shadrick Willis and Ann Wright.
        Elijah Griffith and Nice Dawson.
        Reuben Connerly and Rebekah Pritchett.
     19. Thomas Strangham and Ann Harrington.
November 2. Daniel Sawdon and Eliz^a Broadaway.
        Henry Clift and Eliz^a Cronnoon.
      3. Daniel Edgall and Mary Lowe.
     17. William Keets and Mary Jump.
     18. Thomas Casson and Martha Baynard.
     23. Richard Powell and Ann Kinnamon.
     26. Thomas Ozment and Rachel Sylvester.
     30. Purnell Sylvester and H. Evans.
December 4. James Boggs and Ann Mason.
     16. Anne Cohee and Sarah Sprouse.
     21. William Loveday and Eliza Dudley.
     22. John Bell and Ann Ganatt.
     31. Henry James and Jane Clark.

1779.

January 11. Nicholas Stubbs and Keziah Busick.
     18. Benjamin Faulker and Eliz^a Narvell.
     19. Isaac Nicols and Mary Dean.
February 1. John Barnes and Sarah Chance.

February 3. Allen Thomas and Rhoda Thomas.
   5. Benjamin M‘Kees and Sarah Slaughter.
   6. William Handley and Deborah Harney.
   9. William Frazier and Henrietta Johnson.
  15. Edward Pritchett and Priscilla Minner.
  18. James Gray and Rhoda Dean.
  19. Thomas Orrell and Eliz^a Rumbley.
  22. Wm. Xemar Jr. and Sarah Walker.
  22. William Walker Jr. and Mary Thomas.
  27. James Cochlin and Eliz^a Thompson.
March 2. Levin Parkinson and Rachel Ferriss.
  12. Benjamin Haynes and Sarah Permarr.
  15. Sol. Cahall and Rachel Jones.
April 10. John Valliant Jr. and Eliza Lowrey.
  14. Charles Walker and Sussanna Price.
  14. John Clemments and Rebekah Rogers.
  19. Wm. Walker and Eliz^a Green.
May 17. Nathan Manship and Eleanora Andrews.
  31. John Barrwick and Rachel Webber.
June 3. Robt. Thomas and Eleanor Alford.
  3. Robert Wilson and Eliz^a Pritchett.
  7. Mark Andrews and Ann Manning.
  15. Thomas Chance and Mary Richardson.
  15. Thomas Chance and Rebecca Price.
  15. Nicholas Harrison and Margaret Graham.
  29. Thos Marine and Tamsey Noble.
July 9. John Fields and Esther Meekins.
  12. James Bell and Marg^t Willoughby.
  13. Levi Plummer and Margaret Purnell.
  21. John Ervine and Mary Wadman.
August 6. John Carter and Lydia Hubbert.
  8. William Gall and Mary Scott.
  11. Jeoffrey Horney and Lucretia Scott.
  18. John Wootters and Eliz^a All.
  23. Daniel Crowem Jr. and Rachel Adams.
  25. Uriah Mathews and Polly Lee.
September 7. Tilghman Blades and Ann Lawfull.

September 16. Vincent Lowe Price and Eliz^a Garey.
      19. William Anthony and Eliz^a Haddaway.
      20. Abram Evitt and Mary Stevens.
      29. Nicholas Price and Frances Harris.
October 15. James Baggs and Nancy Mason.
      16. John Nucomb and Mary Swift.
November 2. Robt Pwym and Margaret Reynolds.
      2. James Hobbs and Rachel Reynolds.
      5. Michael Smith and Elizabeth Harris.
      18. John Baker and Sarah Broadaway.
      22. Richd Lockerman and Ann Wood.
December 3. William Perry and Elizabeth Porter.
      10. William Elliott and Sarah Robinson.
      10. Parish Garner and Ann Elliott.
      20. Samuel Douglass and Mary Nevens.
      28. Henry Powell and Dorothy Holland.
      30. Nathl Cooper and Nancy Needels.
      31. Levin Noble and Ann Ward.
      31. Roger Scully and Rachel Harris.

1780.

January 8. Hynson Glanding and Mary Gannon.
      10. David Richards and Tamsey Eaton.
      15. Joseph Durdan and Elizabeth Dickinson.
      19. Greenberry Mathews and Ann Monticue.
February 2. William Love and Elizabeth Parratt.
         James Camper and Sarah Batcheldor.
         William Talboy and Elizabeth Scott.
      7. Charles Scoudrick and Rebekah Wright.
      8. John Robinson and Elizabeth Thorman.
      9. James Black Jr. and Tacy Oldfield.
      12. Samuel Casson and Rebekah Worrell.
      20. Nicholas Bright and Ann Anthony.
      21. John Harrison and Elizabeth Seth.
March 8. Omderton Blades and Sarah Bowdle.
      28. Nicholas Dyall and Mary Dean.
      29. Thomas Leverton and Lydia Calston.

March 29. Isaac Parlett and Jane Hamilton.
April 5. Joseph Stack and Elizabeth Banning.
20. William Fisher and Susannah Webster.
May 9. Thomas Banning and Mary White.
27. Jesse Vinson and Sarah Meredith.
June 21. Roger Fountain and Mary Eaton.
July 17. Mathew Derochbonne and Sarah Wootters.
19. Richard Lyden and Martha Hooper.
August 8. Thomas Mathews and Mary Ann Jackson.
9. Massey Fountain and Henrietta Hicks.
19. Timothy Lane Price and Sarah Parratt.
31. Philemon Downes and Elizabeth Tillotson.
31. Thomas Smith and Nancy White.
September 2. William Jackson and Tryphenia Garrett.
4. Hezekiah Talmon and Ann Story.
11. John Smith and Elonor Anthony.
12. Arthur Clark and Mary Farrowfield.
22. Abner Clemmons and Margaret Morgan.
27. Nathan Gladston and Ann Hobbs.
October 17. Henry Martindale and Nancy Nicols.
George Euberts and Rebecca Herrington.
James Eubanks and Margt. Herrington.
Abel Chilton and Mary Swann.
18. Thomas Hall and Naomi Hammond.
John Corn and Tamsey Rowin.
19. Harrison Monticue and Nancy Lemarr.
John Spurrey and Elizabeth Everett.
James Fountain and Elenor Bell.
27. Richard Warner and Mary Jones.
28. Solomon Carter and Rhoda Webster.
George Morgan and Africa Towers.
November 9. Job Garrett and Priscilla Hignett.
13. Greenbury Mathews and Sarah Pratt.
19. Nath' Harrington and Lydia Nicols.
20. Archibald Jackson and Sukey Reed.
25. Ezekel Dean and Diana Bell.
December 3. William Hutton Jr. and Catharine Jackson.

December 4. John Morgan and Sarah Chaflinch.
 5. Philip Walker and Margaret Dickinson.
 8. Henry Willis and Ann Connerlyd.
 13. Nehemiah Cooper and Elizabeth Morgan.
 17. Benjamin Huggins and Sarah Plummer.
 19. William Webb and Comfort Holson.
 20. Rizdon Bozman and Henrietta Alford.

1781.

January 3. Clousberry Matthews and Mary Slaughter.
 3. Thomas Burk and Elizabeth Turner.
 10. Robert Walker and Sarah Lemarr.
 10. James Cahall and Nelly Dawson.
 13. Benjamin Sutton and Rhode Toottle.
 23. John Salisbury and Lydia Horney.
 25. Edmund Blades and Mary Bownes.
 29. Charles Nenderford and Sarah Moodsley.
 30. John Warren and Ann Western.
February 1. Jacob Wildgoose and Sarah Blades.
 3. John Carpender and Mary Lawrence.
 24. Richard Roe and Sally Glanding.
 26. Richard Mitchell and Sarah Carter.
March 5. John Stevens Jr. and Elizabeth Andrews.
 6. Solomon Morgan and Alice Holdbrook.
 13. Isaac Bradley and Elizabeth Casson.
 16. David Melvill and Sarah Medford.
 20. James Morgan and Justina Cremeen.
April 26. Thomas Turner and Ann Andrew.
May 15. Thomas Cooper Jr. and Elizabeth Colston.
 17. James Morris and Rebecca Barnett.
 29. Ralph Green and Mary Gambell.
June 9. Valentine Green and Jane Sylvester.
 11. John Hardcastle and Jane Potter.
 18. Samuel Southray and Hannah Blades.
 20. Batchelor Chance Jr. and Nancy Dunning.
 " William Fountain and Elizabeth Satterfield.
 21. Robert Orrell and Margaret Bayley.

June 22. John Cooper Jr. and Rachel Conner.
26. David Webber and Mary Andrew.
July 16. John Foster Leverton and Hannah Wilson.
24. John Ryall and Mary Davis.
October 2. James Culbreth and Sarah Covington.
20. Richard Willoughby and Elizabeth Lawrence.
November 1. Solomon Scott and Elizabeth Baggs.
26. Charles Lemarr and Mary Jump.
December 16. James Jones and Susannah Jones.
20. Christopher Wilson and Sarah Dixon.
21. Andrew Bush and Elizabeth Sparklin.

1782.

January 11. Shadrach Dyall and Nancy Horney.
21. Richard Cooper and Sarah Alford.
February 7. Edward Carter and Mary Webb.
24. Thomas J. Condrick and Margaret Monuett.
March 23. William Cecil and Rhoda Skinner.
April 9. Robert Bell and Mary Fountain.
13. John Pippen and Hetty Thornton.
May 22. Wm Robinson and Marg^t Driver.
June 19. Jacob Jump and Lucretia Reed.
29. Wm Andrew and Rachel Pronce.
July 16. John Derochbound and Mary Boone.
August 21. Richard Wootters and Mary Price.
September 10. Henry Turner Jr. and Sarah Blades.
12. Allemby Jump and Nancy Hardcastle.
October 26. John Gibson and Mary Massey.
November 4. James Stafford and Esther Andrews.
December 28. Wm. Meads Satterfield and Ann Dukes.
29. Joseph Bell and Margaret Sewell.

1783.

January 1. Kerrington Sylvester and Sophia Mason.
4. Mathews Garrett and Mary Mason.
20. Howell Kenton and Elizabeth Downes.

January 21. Nathan Harrington and Mary Moborough.

February 26. Richard Mason Jr. and Rebekah Hardcastle.

May 12. Thos. White Meeds and Mary Cooper.

21. John Green and Elizabeth Phillips.

June 5. Samuel Ball and Lydia Kerap.

John Kemp and Ruth Ball.

25. Wm. Fountain and Margaret Morgan.

July 18. John Russum and Tryphena Sylvester.

August 11. Robert Williams and Ann Clark.

September 16. Andrew Satterfield and Deborah Stevens.

October 6. Garey Leverton and Mary Spencer.

10. William Bell Jr. and Margaret Talbott.

10. James Overstock and Elizabeth Perry.

November 12. Samuel Sparklin and Tamsey Andrew.

17. Baptist Davis and Ann Genn.

20. Joseph Parratt and Julia Thomas.

26. James Parratt and Sarah Hutchings.

December 13. John King and Ann Smith.

Richard Willis and Elizabeth Greenbaugh.

15. Charles Critchett and Margaret Webb.

William Coursey Jr. and Mary Thomas.

16. Francis Rowins and Elizabeth Lord.

22. Richard Kinnard and Elizabeth Stanton.

30. Nathan Hill and Rachel Lewis.

1784.

January 14. John Clark and Martha Lyden.

17. Henry Dickinson and Anna Hirdman.

24. Thomas Blades and Keziah Cremeen.

April 6. Thomas Harrington and Rebekah Slaughter.

19. John Diggin and Tamsey Thomas.

28. James Hambleton and Dorothy Ozwell.

May 26. Nathan Smith and Elizabeth Keen.

June 11. James Hardcastle and Sarah Parratt.

27. Zadoc Harvey and Elizabeth Faston.

July 17. Jacob Lockerman and Elizabeth Clark.

August 17. Philip Larcy and Priscilla Lecompt.

August 19. William Walter and Nancy Driver.
　　　　30. Thomas Baynard Jr. and Rebeckah Sangston.
October 19. Mathew Chilton and Hannah Wootters.
　　　　20. James Ratcliff and Mary Alls.
November 2. George Nelson and Margaret Stradley.
　　　　16. Thomas Tootle and Sarah Brown.
　　　　19. William Cannon and Henrietta Wheatley.
　　　　　Solomon Jump and Sarah Cannon.
　　　　　Noah Mason and Izabel Hunter.

1785.

January 3. William Mason and Nancy Baggs.
　　　　20. John Fisher and Katharine Holt.
　　　　27. Abner Clements and Lydia Stewart.
February 2. Jonathan Gary and Sousana Dickinson.
　　　　8. George Wilson and Sally Cooper.
　　　　22. Ezekel Hunter Jr. and Prudence Boone.
　　　　23. Peter Chance and Rebecca Boone.
March 6. John Harrison and Elizth. Scissarson.
　　　　9. Eliza[?] Clark and Elizabeth Robinson.
　　　　12. Samuel Denny and Anna Montecue.
　　　　16. Thomas Roe and Tilly Porter.
　　　　18. Giles Hicks and Margaret Chalmers.
April 26. Thomson Wootters and Elizabeth Jarman.
May 3. Richard Swift and Sarah Reynolds.
　　　　30. John Blades and Lucretia Turner.
June 7. Thomas Purnell and Katharine Hargidine.
　　　　14. Charles Baker and Frances Willis.
July 14. Henry Calston and Rebecca Mason.
　　　　15. Levin Thomas and Elizabeth Ganze.
　　　　16. Edwin Lunceford and Sarah Kelley.
　　　　29. Robert Sherwin and Mary Mobray.
August 17. Aaron Lewis and Sapphira Griffith.
　　　　18. Thomas Lewis Jr. and Rebecca Griffith.
　　　　23. Richard Perry and Deborah Sitterson.
　　　　26. William Dail and Nancy Barnes.

September 21. Samuel Darggins and Ann Johnston.
October 5. Mathias Freeman and Juliet Dudley.
11. James Johnson and Elizabeth Russum.
November 25. Alexander McConnell and Dorothy Le Compte.
December 9. William Purnell Jr. and Elizabeth Cooper.
27. John Townsend and Sarah Slaughter.
" James Fleharty and Susannah Hopkins.
28. James Wilson and Sarah Cooper.

1786.

January 9. William Kelley and Roxanna Wing.
18. Griffith Callahan and Ann Wood.
19. Olive[?] Jump and Mary Wootters.
26. Samuel Sylvester and Sarah Phillips.
31. Isaac Baggs and Elizabeth Clark.
March 12. Wm. Everingham and Elizabeth Willis.
April 19. Stephen Cooper and Priscilla Scott.
May 15. James Coblins and Sarah Perry.
16. Andrew Jump and Letitia Boon.
20. George Townsend and Margaret Bell.
June 19. John Robertson and Margaret Stevens.
23. Josiah Leach and Alice Parratt.
July 8. James Mathews and Margaret Oram.
15. Solomon Colbourn and Rebecca Coursey.
December 18. Nathan Sewell and Elizabeth Norris.
22. Charles Manship and Mary Keene.
" Edward Dudley and Rebecca Colston.
27. Giles Hiche and Mary Colston.
28. Daniel Jones and Cleah Cannon.

1787.

January 9. William Kirby and Sarah Haddaway.
16. John Freeman and Margaret Clark.
27. Benjamin Boone and Ann Hall.
29. Daniel Valliant and Elizabeth Alford.
February 8. Elijah Andrews and Mary Noble.

February 16. John Cremen and Rebecca Lynch.
          18. James Aaron and Grace Wildgood.
March 12. Ellis Thomas and Mary Harris.
        15. Henry Dickinson and Deborah Perry.
        19. John Royall and Ann Evans.
        21. John Slaughter and Elizabeth Hynson.
April 5. Thomas Hitchings and Fanny Reynolds.
        6. James Jump and Elizabeth Ridgaway.
       16. William Parker and Elizabeth Nicols.
May   8. Henry Covington and Susanna Boone.
June 20. James Hardcastle and Elizabeth Baggs.
July 14. John Cooper and Sarah Cooper.
       17. James Love and Rebecca Eagle.
       25. Robert Sylvester and Rebecca Boone.
August 11. James Turner and Ann Elliott.
        28. James Cohee and Mary Brice.
September 5. Samuel Collins and Deborah Satterfield.
         25. Francis Elliott and Elizabeth Orrell.
         26. William Ryon and Sarah Alford.
October 9. James Slaughter and Priscilla Harrington.
November 3. James Grayless and Elizabeth Wheatley.
        12. Benoin Sherwin and Ann Stradley.
        13. Richard Collison and Penelope Bush.
        19. Solomon Brown and Ann Boon.
        24. Isaac Nicols and Celia Wright.
        28. Caleb Kerby and Margaret Shields.
December 1. Robert Hardcastle and Susanah Garey.
         8. James Leverton and Lydia Kenton.

1788.

January 22. Richard Willis and Bethany Gwoty.
February 2. Jacob Seth and Ann Pennington.
         7. Thos. Whadman and Henrietta Yoe.
        10. William Sherwood and Sarah Mitchell.
April   3. Richard Andrew and Mary Hill.
June   10. Aaron Hardcastle and Arabella Stokely.
        13. James Munnett and Mary Kenderdine.

June 13. James Sleete and Ann Manship.
  14. James Harrington and Ann McKinny.
  27. William Harper and Amelia Holden.
July 26. Jacob Boon and Catharine Whitby.
August 1. John Roe and Elizabeth Rawley.
  5. Noah Mason and Nancy Jackson.
  6. Mathew Jones and Sarah White.
  7. Edward Andrew and Prudence Walker.
  16. Richard Clarkson and Priscilla Brown.
  25. Owen Connelly and Elizabeth Layton.
  " Jonathan Hughey and Ann Robinson.
  31. John Barcross and Sarah Hayes.
September 3. Jacob Andrew and Priscilla Law.
October 21. Robert Dixon and Ann Andrew.
  28. Rizdon Fountain and Rachel Saulsbury.
November 8. Henry Downes and Margaret Green.
  12. James Towers Jr. and Mary Hobbs.
  " James Towers and Tamsey Bland.
  15. Perry Sutton and Nancy Dawson.
  18. James Cheezum and Nancy Tottel.
  20. Burton Loftis and Sussana Baynard.
  28. Richard Start and Ann Harris.

1789.

February 8. Elijah Williamson and Lely Wheatley.
  24. Benjamin Jackson and Rebecca Parrott.
March 9. William Lane and Sarah George.
  11. Perry Young and Rachel Stack.
  13. Henry Kemp and Mary Layton.
  18. Josiah Starling and Amelia Nicols.
  30. Levin Noble and Mary White Ward.
April 12. John Scott and Ann Talboy.
May 29. William Vaulx and Mary Tumpillian.
  30. Alexander Talson and Rebecca Boon.
June 19. John Shepherd and Fanny Foster.
July 14. Robert Postlethwaite and Nancy Kenton.
  27. James Meredith and Anna Statia Ewing.

July 28. Thos. Baynard and Elizabeth Slaughter.
  29. Robt. Edge and Mary Pynfield.
August 5. John Flowers and Elizabeth Clank.
  11. James Kenton and Sarah Micton.
  15. Ralph Colscott and Mary Swiggett.
  18. James Swann and Lydia Faulkner.
  24. Francis Sellers and Elizabeth Downes.
  29. John Harrison and Esther Blades.
September 8. James Fountain and Margaret Saulsbury.
  12. Jonathan Stevens and Frances Hignitt.
  15. Daniel Herring and Rachel Cohee.
  19. John Willoughby and Celia Connelly.
  " James Faulker and Sophia Minner.
  29. Wm. Wheatley and Sidney Glandon.
October 3. Charles Blair and Ann Stevens.
  " John Merchant and Phener Jackson.
  9. James Purnell and Elizabeth Neal.
  " Daniel Dawson and Ann Willis.
  " Daniel Bell and Ann Coulbourn.
November 2. Thomas Slaughter and Mary Kelly.
  13. John Brown and Fanney Coursey.
  19. George Martin and Elizabeth Nicols.
  29. James Beaver and Ann Hughes.
December 2. John Minner Jr. and Elizabeth Nunam.
  24. William Clift and Elizabeth Broadway.
  28. Joshua Lucas and Deborah Willis.

1790.

January 5. Peter Collison and Sarah Johnson.
  14. Luke Andrew and Rhody Blades.
  16. Thomas White Brown and Lucretia Cannon.
  30. Abraham Ross and Elizabeth Green.
February 2. Thomas Baxter and Mary Hughes.
  3. Philip Thomas and Sarah James.
  16. John Quinn and Elizabeth Townsend.
March 2. Jeremiah Montigue and Elizabeth Clough.
  3. Noah Dawson and Margaret Andrew.

March 5. John Martindale and Mary Manship.
13. William Harrison and Penelope Collison.
19. Emory Craynor and Susannah Lyon.
23. George Garey and May Andrew.
April 2. Perry Ward Stewart and Mary Manship.
" John Salterfield and Sarah Williams.
7. Robert Boon and Sarah Hunter.
10. Thomas Bright and Nelly Robinson.
17. Risdon Cooper and Elizabeth Mace.
21. Peter Taylor Causey and Elizabeth Wilson.
22. John Lucas and Rebecca Cooper.
May 3. Jesse Grayless and Sarah Andrew.
11. Purnell Jump and Elizabeth Broadaway.
12. John Green and Sarah Smith.
17. Bennnett Wherrett and Rebecca Scott.
18. William Diggins and Margaret Chairs.
25. Abraham Ray and Nancy Travers.
June 7. William Richardson Jr. and Elizabeth Dickinson.
July 9. Richard Wilcott and Rebecca Cheezam.
20. Elsbury Burt and Sarah Hutchings.
25. Ezekel Hunter and Sarah Sylvester.
27. John Hutchings and Fanny Harrington.
August 3. Elijah Pitsham and Elizabeth Swift.
5. John Waddell and Elizabeth Wright.
12. Jonathan Conner and Della Crickett.
17. David Webber and Catharine Isgate.
20. Hugh Lindsey and Mary Caulk.
September 3. Vincent Pinkine and Catharine Cooper.
John Lucas and Caroline Scott.
October 1. John Fleharty and Esther Hopkins.
21. Samuel Johnson and Hannah Jackson.
November 2. John Bradley and Rebecca Jump.
5. John Jump and Henrietta Lee.
6. David Jones and Tamsey Connerty.
10. Levin Claudge and Rachel Jump.
Benjamin Linthicum and Rebecca Dixon.

November 11. Timothy Plummer and Sarah Vickers.
John Bowdle and Mary Towers.
12. Isaac Purnill and Patty Sylvester.
December 10. William Andrew and Margaret Beauchamp.
13. Joseph Crockett and Rebecca Blades.
14. Thomas Swift and Sarah Mason.
15. William Jacobs and Mary Dawson.
22. James Chairs Webb and Nancy Hicals.

1791.

January 1. William Gibson and Elizabeth Sangston.
2. Joseph Stack and Rebecca Lewis.
3. James Sisk and Mary Bowdle.
4. Henry Mason and Mary Clark.
Archibald Flemming and Sarah Wilson.
11. Alexander Forsyth and Margaret Smith.
14. Henry Turner Jr. and Rebecca Eaton.
18. John Adams and Mary Russom.
Joshua Temple and Nancy Wilson.
27. John Morgan and Sarah Clift.
31. William Bright and Elizabeth Shephard.
February 4. Jacob Watkins and Elizabeth Hobbs.
7. William Shaw and Polly Sylvester.
8. William Crafford and Ann Harbert.
12. Henry Casson and Polly Nabb.
12. Joseph Bowdel and Polly Blades.
15. John Fountain Jr. and Deborah Fountain.
23. Saml. Willoughby and Amelia Howard.
March 3. Alexander —— and Nancy Price.
5. Woshuan Hughey and Polly Johnson.
7. John Seth and Nancy Meredith.
8. John Martindale and Margaret Saulsbury.
15. John Dodd and Polly Jump.
22. Thomas Clen Denning and Hannah Burt.
31. Thomas Katts and Polly Waddell.
April 6. Caleb Bouvier and Sidney Harrington.
28. William Dail and Mary Eaton.

May   3. Joseph Dixon and Ann With.
   5. Peter Edmordson and Elizabeth Driver.
   23. James Dudley and Mary Burton.
June   1. Daniel Keene and Margaret Bill.
   11. John Dickinson and Ann Walker.
   30. Nehemiah Townsend and Winifred Fountain.
July   8. Nichalson Harrison and Hester Hall.
   17. Thos. Frampton and Elizabeth Kelly.
   21. Joshua Hobbs and Rhody Cranmer.
   27. William All and Isabel Boon.
   30. Samuel Lecompte and Sarah Benney.
August   3. Benjamin Jump and Sidney Carter.
   6. Daniel Hobbs and Elizabeth White.
November 17. Robert Walker and Margaret Valliant.
   18. Levin Hicks and Elizabeth Stewart.
   20. Tristram Wright and Elizabeth Waddell.
   22. Samuel Chatman and Sarah Nunam.
   23. Nehemiah Andrew and Anna Davis.
   28. Emanuel Crayner and Susannah Wadman.
December 18. Acquilla Jackson and Penelope Biscow.
   20. John Watkins and Elizabeth Ruhard.

1792.

January   3. Thomas Cooper and Elizabeth Whirritt.
   Elijah Satterfield and Elizabeth Dukes.
   William Dukes and Lydia Harris.
   4. James Anderson and Celia Harris.
   9. Thomas Smith and Rhody Cooper.
   17. Barnett McCombs and Sarah Sunarr.
   20. Solomon Dennis Cranor and **Elizabeth Morriston.**
   26. Richard Harrington and Rebecca Harrington.
February 14. Levin Saulsbury and Mary Cremun.
   15. James Ewing and Elizabeth Griffith.
   " James Peters and Sarah Hignult.

February 21. James Whiteley and Rebecca Culbreth.
" Solomon Atkinson and Mary Kenton.
March 8. Aaron Dut and Ann Dawson.
22. John Hendsley and Sarah Clark.
April 3. Daniel Holbrook and Rebecca Towers.
4. Solomon Wilson and Elizabeth Craynor.
25. Zadwick Lain and Amelia Gray.
May 19. Solomon Richardson and Mary Moberry.
June 1. James Waddell and Mary Saulsbury.
5. Zebulon Dixon and Nancy Garrett.
Jonathan Wilson and Mary Saulsbury.
James Wheatley and —— ——.
19. David Webber and Mary Ann Wootters.
26. Henry Garmon and Sarah Bush.
Nehemiah Draper and Sidney Barwick.
July 24. Richard Martindale and Sarah Martindale.
Thomas Harvey and Nelly Beadley.
27. William Wadman and Nancy Craynor.
31. Henry Baggs and Elizabeth Roe.
August 7. Isaac Boon and Ann Boon.
21. William Clough and Elizabeth Monticue.
Isaac Merrick and Rachel Sylvester.
29. George Collins and Nice Hubbert.
September 15. Aaron Dawley and Nancy Purnell.
25. Levin Charles and Henrietta Thaughley.
Henry Kenton and Lydia Downes.
October 17. Owen McQuality and Jane Harris.
27. John Jones and Sarah Caulk.
November 13. James Wilson and Elizabeth Hardcastle.
James Boon and Sarah Boon.
December 8. James Plummer and Letitia Clift.
14. Nathan Jones and Rebecca Swift.
Dovington Chane and Esther Gosling.
18. William Mobrary and Rhoda Ross.
John Carter Jr. and Lavinia Rumbley.
20. Robinson Morriston and Ann Hignutt.
22. Joseph Fleharty and Margaret Cook.

December 22. Thomas Truman and Sarah Kinimint.
   25. Robert Meredith and Nancy Chance.

1793.

January 3. Jacob Covey and Mary Camper.
  22. James Coarsey and Rebecca Harper.
  29. Edward White 3rd and Elizabeth Fountain.
  30. William Walker and Rebecca Crunan.
February 7. Stephen Theodore Johnson and Mary Clarke.
  12. John Ball and Fanny Vinson.
March 23. Solomon Brown and Parthena Furnis.
   Noah Jackson and Elizabeth Smith.
  23. Levin Tute and Deborah Eaton.
May 2. Israel Knotts and Sarah Martindall.
  17. Richard Ridgeway and Henny Townsend.
  20. Aaron Manship and Nancy Mathews.
  28. Samuel Barron and Marthy Cox.
   William Casson and Letitia Swift.
  30. Henry Stewart and Sarah Foster.
June 4. Elisha Chalfinch and Mary Craynor.
  12. Henry Willis and Rhody Batchelor.
  21. Richard Pearson and Deborah Hopkins.
July 20. Mathias Clifton and Eliza Blunt.
  23. Thomas Stewart and Polly Collinson.
  24. Greenberry Banning and Nancy Clarke.
August 9. Saml. Fountain and Sarah Lawrence.
  13. Richard Swift and Rachel Smith.
  14. Solomon Clarke and Sarah Swift.
  20. Thomas Winchester and Nancy Priort.
September 27. Thomas Mason and Eliza Saven.
November 19. William Potter and Ann Richardson.
  22. Roger Malock and Sarah Dill.
  26. John Cheshire and Rachel Martindall.
December 16. Thomas Webster and Sarah Smith.
  18. Nicholas Linch and Mary Ruse.
  20. Thomas Bartlett and Mary Thomas.
  21. Cornelius Johnson and Sarah Brannock.

3

December 21. William Wheeler and Mary Lyden.
    24. Christopher Pratt and Rebecca Trunen.
    26. Edward Perry and Elizabeth Walker.
    30. Joseph Rogers and Frances Smith.
    30. Levin Crossman and Sarah Collins.
    31. Nathaniel Stafford and Sarah Hobbs.

1794.

January 6. Benedict Numan and Rachel Benson.
    14. Thomas Carslake and Margaret Luse.
    15. John Harris and Seina Willis.
    21. Isaac Munnitt and Rebecca Chilton.
February 1. David Dean and Elizabeth Moore.
    5. Ephraim Grayless and Peggy Wheatley.
    11. Robert Sylvester and Frances Boon.
        Philip Porter and Rebecca Glass.
    12. James Draper and Levis White.
    20. John Claredge and Rachel Smith.
    22. Benjamin Todd and Mary Harvey.
    25. Henry Rhodes and Rachel Simmons.
    27. William Waddell and Nancy Cheezum.
March 1. Henry Nicols 3rd. and Margaret Keene.
    11. Andrew Kinneman and Christian Keene.
    20. William Colston and Mary Debilbiss.
April 17. John Sylvester and Prudence Sundick.
    25. Daniel Baynard and Nancy Parrott.
        William Starkey and Deborah Gibson.
June 5. William Hignutt and Ann Dillon.
    11. William Taylor and Elizabeth Faulkner.
    16. John Knus and Sarah Sumners.
    17. Jo'n Shepperd and Sarah Eaton.
    20. Robert Hefferson and Judith Pennarr.
July 19. Charles Sebudrach and Sarah Cocklin.
    21. John Fluharty and Eliza Vallant.
        Samuel Emerson and Ann Anderson.
    23. Wm. Kirkman and Eliza Spurry.
    26. Vincent Taylor and Elizabeth Martindall.

July 26. Thomas Andran and Heziah Blades.

August 1. William Faris and Luvenah Alford.

    13. John Ward and Sarah Grayloss.

    19. John Peters and Mary Hignutt.

       Mathew Smith and Eliza Ewing.

       Joseph Mann and Eliza Blades.

    20. John A Sangston and Mary Kenton.

September 5. Solomon Diggins and Rachel Condon.

    8. Thomas Towers and Esther Collins.

       Ja⁵ Minner and Darkey Faulkner.

November 17. John Green and Elizabeth Smill.

    28. Wm. Ryon Jr. and Nancy Graham.

December 2. John Grigg and Cynthia Minner.

    18. Wm. Reeves and Mary Taylor.

    23. William Travers and Jann Haslett.

    31. Thomas Griffith and Darkey Eaton.

1795.

January 3. James McKnitt and Julia Robinson.

    8. James Wiltegott and Nancy Flaharty.

       " Thos. Waddell and Sarah Batchelor.

    13. William Priest and Naomi Carmine.

       William Harper and Sarah Carmine.

    29. Samuel Elliott and Hannah Clark.

February 14. Jas. Anderson and Nancy Jackson.

April 4. William Ross and Margaret Kelley.

June 18. John Diggins and Elizabeth Cooper.

    20. Thomas Tylor and Mary Alford.

    22. Amos Warren and Wealthy Baynord.

July 4. Thomas Hawkins and Ada Borjan.

    17. Robt. Beauchamp and Mary Wilson.

    29. Thomas Berry and Jaminah Pratt.

August 5. Richard Dove and Esther Chilcut.

    13. Joshua Cooper and Lydia Clark.

    15. Nehemiah Andrew and Phœba Sutton.

       William Keene and Rebecca Floyd.

    20. William Webb and Rachel Diggins.

August 20. James Bell and Isabella Jump.
　　　　　John Hughbanks and Esther Ridgeway.
　　　　　Levin Clark and Elizabeth Niec.
　　　　　Henry Garey and Abigail Chilton.
September 7. Sol. Hubbert and Africa Russnur.
　　　　　30. Cain Davis and Mary Carter.
October 28. Tam Cerlan D. Sangston and Mary Stevens.
November 17. Daniel Morgan and Sarah Towers.
　　　　　Edward Carter Sr. and Lela Jones.
　　　　　24. James Stewart and Esther Pratt.
　　　　　28. Callahan Jones and Rebecca Carmine.
December 2. Thomas Carmine and Lovey Harris.
　　　　　9. Wm. Hardcastle and Mary Jump.
　　　　　15. Wm. Towers and Celia Russell.
　　　　　15. Rigby Thomas and Delilah Barnett.
　　　　　19. Thomas Meeds and Mary Swift.
　　　　　22. Aaron Chance and Sarah Love.

1796.

January 11. David Waddell and Elizabeth Brannock.
　　　　　12. Geo. Thompson and Henny Kenton.
　　　　　19. Levi Dukes and Deborah Saulsbury.
　　　　　21. Jonathan Beck and Rebecca Nicol.
　　　　　22. Daniel Wooters and Elizabeth Wooters.
February 2 Robert Pearce and Sarah Hardcastle.
　　　　　9. Alun Parker and Rhody Willis.
　　　　　20. Thos. Beauchamp and Mary Todd.
　　　　　23. Ezekiel Murdock and Rutha Ireland.
　　　　　Robt. Hefferson and Letitia Porter.
March 5. William Slaughter and Susannah Rhodes.
　　　　　7. James Swiggett and Ann Harrington.
　　　　　15. Tilghman Chance and Ann Harper.
　　　　　30. Thomas Priest and Aisey Jump.
　　　　　John Murphy and Susannah Slaughter.
April 14. Robert Williams and Mary Stunnors.
　　　　　16. Absalom Tribitt and Ann Draper.
May 17. Henry Dean and Tamsey Covey.

May 25. Mark Foster and Eleoner Cole.
   30. Andrew McCollorton and Mary Vauly.
June 22. William Shehan and Sarah Sylvestor.
   25. David Sylvestor and Elinor Tarrorsfold.
July 19. Asa Brady and Nancy Hollingsworth.
August 6. John Orom and Mary Edgell.
   10. Andrew Baggs and Henrietta Mason.
   13. David Sisk and Elizabeth Foster.
   16. Thomas Cooper and Rebecca Nobb.
     Jeremiah Vinson and Prudence Hunter.
   30. Melvon Andrews and Celia Andrew.
   31. John A. Sangston and Rachel Sharp.
September 6. Richard Warner and Parthy Nelson.
     S. Talbott and Ann Postlethwaite.
   24. Thomas Carmine and Susannah Andrew.
     Thomas Monticue and Hannah Dodd.
   26. Joseph Wright and Anna Hatia Meredith.
   26. Jacob Numar and Nancy Cotrile.
October 10. Nathan Whitby and Mary Fountaine.
   11. Peter Chance and Elenor Farrfield.
     Harrison Montigue and Triphemia Fountain.
   12. Anderson Porter and Bershiba Jester.
   15. Robt. Hardcastle Jr and Sarah Baynord
   26. John Cantor and Margaret Fountain.
November 8. Shelby Jump and Elizabeth Jump.
December 3. Elijah Cromean and Ann Dawson.
   10. David Wilson and Mary Williams.
   13. William Rumble and Margaret Perry.
   27. William Warren and Lovie Draper.
   28. Levin Swiggett and Peggy Forsythe.

1797.

January 3. James Dixon and Henrietta Vinson.
     James Herring and Cynthia Chance.
   5. Philip Rhodes and Mary Cony.
     William Boone and Elizabeth Driver.

January 9. John Monticue and Rachel Roe.
        17. Joa. C. Willowby and Sophia Beauchamp.
        23. Levin Hobbs and Sarah Roe.
        31. William Young and Mary Dewoohburne.
February 3. Amos Hollingsworth and Lucretia Bradley.
         6. Amasa Robinson and Mary Nicols Douglass.
         7. Edward Price and Mary George.
            Andrew Price and Sarah Brine.
        21. Wm. M'Comakin and Mary Robinson.
        22. Joshua Soward and Robena Johnson.
            Stephen Trusty and Alice Carnoy.
            Nehemiah Saulsbury and Sarah Koons.
March 11. Stephen Lucas and Elizabeth Gibson.
      29. John Scribner and Robena Collins.
April 4. John Ireland and Esther Johnson.
          Daniel Swiggett and Sallie Clarke.
May   2. P. Martindall and Elizabeth Orton.
       4. Thomas Daffin and Rebecca Dickinson.
      24. Nehemiah Riley and Susanna White.
      26. Thomas Orem and Julia Taylor.
      30. Josiah Genn and Rachel Hardcastle.
      31. Thomas Jump and Nancy King.
June 13. Nicholas Loveday and Mary Shirwood.
     24. William Miller and Ann Manship.
     26. Philemon Spencer and Nancy Baggs.
     27. Joshua Craynor and Rhoda Eaton.
July 4. John Nabb and Susanna Jaickson.
     12. Charles Citizen and Sarah Tholley.
     16. Richard Small and Letty Ross.
     30. William Swift and Addah Swift.
August 1. Nathan Hunter and Susanna Cox.
      10. John Stanton and Elizabeth Connolly.
      16. Peter Mathews and Ann M'Gram.
      28. John Faiross and Nancy Blades.
      31. George Bland and Elizabeth Caulk.
September 1. Horatio Sharpe and Prissilla Pritchett.
          25. Johnson Hobbs and Sarah Griffith.

October 2. Pritchett Ross and Rhoda Wright.
      9. Waitman Gaslin and Margaret Causey.
    24. Peter Sharpe and Elizabeth Fountain.
    27. Joseph Eaton and Rachel Prouce.

Book No. 3.

November 1. Henry Harrington and Nancy Catrap.
    4. Caleb Clarke and Prudence Taylor.
    8. Francis Davis and Elizabeth Genn.
   22. Solomon Cannon and Rebecca Mason.
   27. James Jakes and Elizabeth Webber.
December 11. Abidnigo Bodfield and Nancy Chilton.
    12. Peter Hardcastle and Mary Baynard.
    16. John Rumble and Parentha Blades.
    19. Samuel Alford and Barsheba Kelly.
    " Manapy Koon and Elenor Stewart.
    20. Zackariah Gowty and Lucretia Andrew.
    27. Robt. McPherson and Mary Walker.
    27. James Smith and Minty Russell.

1798.

January 2. Philemon Harrington and Lydia Parrott.
    3. Cain Davis and Nancy Stubbs.
    6. Able Griffith and Allopia Andrews.
    8. Isaiah Blades and Ritta Connerly.
    9. Jonathan Stewart and Margaret Walker.
   11. Robert Sylvester and Sidney Jump.
   11. Purnell Sylvester and Esther Jump.
   12. John Barwick and Deborah Roe.
   16. Moses Boon and Polly Sylvester.
   23. Thos. Coursey and Margaret Sylvester.
   25. Thos. Wootters and Dorothy Williams.
   29. Charles Dean and Sarah Turnor.
   31. Daniel Dukes and Sarah Evitts.
February 3. Levin Blades and Rosannah Kelley.
    22. James Vinson and Rebeccah Henly.
    27. Jeremiah Nicols and Kitty Andrews.

February 27. Levin Williams and Sarah Wright.
March 5. Joshua Listor and Barbary Kid.
    7. Henry Hill and Mary Girrald.
   15. Peter Rich and Prudence Lane.
   22. Alex. Maxwell Jr. and Eliza Gibson.
   27. William Young and Eliza Loveday.
April 13. Richard Harrington and Mary Casson.
   18. Charles White and Margaret Fiddeman.
May 8. James Henigatt and Remis Fountain.
   15. Noah Mason and Margaret Bell.
June 2. William Todd and Nancy Griflith.
   12. William Prusk and Nancy Merrick.
   13. Nicholas Benson and Mary Kinnamont.
   15. Richard Griffith and Lydia ——.
   16. Owen Cooper and Lydia Dwiggins.
   25. Nehemiah Causey and Ann Pitisy.
July 3. Seth Hill Evitts and Rebecca Wilson.
   20. Lemuel Cahee and Rachel Hargadine.
   24. Robinson Stevens and Jane Collins.
   25. Samuel Davidson and Deborah Ross.
   28. Nicholas Hopkins and Rebecca Perry.
August 2. Cyrus Bell and Sarah Dawson.
   6. William Colliston and Sarah Stevens.
   30. John Wright and Ann Webb.
September 3. Marmaduke Spencer and Sarah Sieth.
   14. Ross Thompson and Polly Dudley.
   " William Dillahay and Ada Harris.
   24. George Newtner and Mary Swift.
   29. Richard Handcock and Rebecca Pinder.
October 1. Peter Wright and Esther Ross.
   George Sewell and Nancy Hopkins.
   3. William Berridge and Sarah Piterkin.
   4. Thomas Baker and Rebecca Andrews.
   16. Thomas Gannon and Sarah Harper.
   17. Thomas Pearson and Peggy Lane.
   23. James Webber and Mary Farrowfield.
   24. Owen Boon and Elizabeth Robinson.

October 27. Cornelius Towers and Elizabeth Carmine.
" Nathan Bourke and Sarah Noling.
November 5. Edward Swift and Hannah Boon.
13. Thomas Bartlett and Biddy Prince.
19. William Black and Elizabeth Lyon.
28. William Harris and Elizabeth Carter.
December 4. John Towers and Elizabeth Stubbs.
6. Thomas Jewell and Terressa Jester.
18. Samuel Culbreth and Susannah Smothers.
19. James Ward and Lucretia Dawson.
19. James Breeding and Anna Gibson.
20. James Hunter and Deborah Harvey.
26. John Gary and Hester Whitby.
28. Thomas Bartlete and Mary Eaton.
31. James Jones and Rachel Clarke.

1799.

January 4. Peter Jump and Mary Jump.
" John Lane and Elizabeth Manship.
" Thomas Withgatt and Elizabeth Orem.
8. William Young and Henrietta Montigue.
Andrew Beachamp and Fanny Eaton.
Isaac Lee and Ann Stidham.
15. John Knots and Cynthia Gouty.
" William A. Cooper and Ann George.
16. Thomas Kidd and Lydia Manship.
22. James Hubbard and Charlotte Breeding.
22. Thomas Wing and Sarah Duhadaway.
" Jesse Turner and Elizabeth Ewing.
23. James Harrison and Alice Delahay.
William Emerson and Dorothy Waddell.
28. Solomon Minner and Rebecca Herd.
John Richardson and Susan Ewing.
February 1. William Gray and Nancy Jump.
" Moses Cohe and Sarah Maltee.
4. William Manship and Nancy Thorp.
6. Arthur Travers and Nancy Rich.

4

February 11. James Barwick and Nancy Roe.
       13. Thos. Hardcastle and Sarah Pearce.
       19. Wm. Satterfield and Elizabeth Mark.
       " Andrew Peters and Mary Ann Breeding.
       26. James Price and Ann Kenton.
       William B. Whitby and Sarah Boon.
March 6. William Loftas and Elizabeth Mounticue.
       12. Isaac Chance and Sarah Chance.
       —— Flemming and Araminta Willis.
       13. Nathan Russell and Nancy Sparkes.
       21. George Price and Nancy Dwiggins.
       27. James Russum and Deborah Plummer.
April 9. Edward Fountain and Fanny Bent.
       19. Sewell Handy and Harriott Hutchings.
       23. William Bradley and Esther Cooper.
       30. Robert Marshall and Nancy Cohee.
May 13. Solomon Bartlett and Mary Nunam.
June 1. Joseph Price and Sarah Bordley.
       21. John Blunt and Sarah Malony.
       25. Zebulon Hopkins and Sarah Barwick.
       26. William Hopkins and Anna Lyden.
       27. John Eagle and Sarah Townsend.
July 4. Turburt Kern and Hester Hynson.
       20. Clemont Wheelen and Peggy Starky.
       26. James Corrie and Mary Downes.
       27. Edgar Andrew and Anna Wright.
August 4. Edward Barwick and Sarah Jump.
       14. Benjamin Roe and Betsy Bodfield.
       26. Robert Peters and Tamsey Eaton.
       " Richard Lyden and Betsey Fountain.
September 3. James Stevans and Mary Dillon.
       24. Zebedee Whiteley and Esther Wright.
       " William Lucas and Sarah Hubbard.
       26. Anderton Carmine and Elizabeth Fisher.
October 2. John Russam and Ann ——.
       17. John Smoot and Elizabeth Douglass.
       21. John Moore and Sarah Fleharty.

November 7. John M. Beath and Elizabeth Whiteley.
          9. Emory Sylvester and Tilly Blunt.
December 2. Francis Mastin and Rebecca Farrele.
          3. Nicholas Stubbs and Nancy Pattison.
       10. James Thowley and Mary Porter.
       12. Joseph Cromean and Polly Malcom.
       16. Cain Andrew and Sarah Willis.
       17. Elijah Strodley and Lydia Minner.
       23. Solomon Swann and Sarah Teat.
           Jabez Caldwell and Sarah Hardcastle.
           Thomas Saulsbury and Nancy Downes.

1800.

January 1. William Ross and Ann Causey.
        8. Thomas Harding and Bethany ——.
          Egdell Scondrach and Sally Edgell.
     14. Thomas Reynolds and Frances Smith.
     16. W^m. Vickers and Ritty Pritchett.
     18. Jeremiah Rhodes and Sarah Cooper.
     22. Andrew Covey and Sarah Morgan.
     24. Robert Jordan and Dorcas Hopkins.
February 8. John Hancock and Sally Boon.
     17. Henry Coursey and Rachel Merrick.
March 18. William Elliott and Rebecca Banoick.
          Daniel Stevens and Juliana Waddell.
     25. John Lee and Nancy Boon.
April 7. Joshua Lucas and Elizabeth Valliant.
     29. Stephen Lucas and Leah Lecompte.
May 1. James Harris and Lovey Parker.
     13. John Cooper and Lydia Cooper.
     " Thomas Garrett and Nancy Frampton.
     17. William Plummer and Rebecca Booker.
     20. John Corrie and Rachel ——.
June 16. Hezekiah Satterfield and Peggy Diggins.
     22. George Price and Nancy Williamson.
July 29. Thomas Jones and Ann Hollingsworth.
     30. Levin Wright and Mary Ward.

August   2. John Cooper and Sarah Smith.
      20. Samuel Lyons and Dorcas Craynor.
      26. Miles Hearnes and Sarah Glandon.
September 3. Robert Stewart and Nancy Chance.
      11. Charles Case and Precilla Mereditts.
      22. Joseph Vickers and Betsy Davis.
      23. Josiah Genn and Margaret Barker.
October 28. Andrew Oram and Elizabeth ——.
November 4. John Clough and Hannah Prate.
       8. Peregrine Byard and Arabella Hardcastle.
      11. Elijah Barwick and Ann Evitts.
      12. Giles Hicks and Nancy Fountaine.
      15. Joseph Talbot and Elizabeth Mason.
      29. John Clark and Christiana O'Donald.
      29. Solomon Brown and Hester Boon.
December 3. Nathaniel Sitterfield and Nisah Caball.
       8. Peter Thilcute and Polly Dean.
      12. Paul Connaway and Priscilla Gauslin.
      13. Edmond Farrele and Elizabeth Winchester.
      17. John Council and Patty Clemants.
      20. John Ashland and Elizabeth Welsh.
      22. White B. Smith and Airey Brown.
      24. John Street and Mary Herrin.
      29. Joseph W. Cerod and Rachel Birth.

1801.

January 3. Thomas Fountain and Mary Manship.
       3. Levi Burt and Sally Swift.
       6. Ephraim Faulkner and Esther Harrowfield.
       6. Garritson Waddle and Elizabeth Fisher.
      11. Peter Hubbord and Mary Collins.
      12. John Martindale and Charlotte Montague.
      17. James Black and Rachel Swift.
      23. Sanders Griflin and Mary Sherman.
      24. James Nicols and Elizabeth Blades.
      24. James Wilson and Lydia Baynard.
      27. Henry Garey and Hannah Sylvester.
      30. Neils Neall and Lydia ——.

February 3. William Dillin and Nancy Morgan.
      " Nathan Plumer [?] and Sarah Boon.
February 4. Alex. Able and Rebecca Reed.
     12. James Price and Mary Richardson.
     24. Elbert Downes and Ann Chilcott.
     28. John Dougherty and Prudence Fountain.
March 10. Stanton Carroll and Sarah Manship.
     14. Anderton Blades and Randle Towers.
April 1. William Cafran and Milly Snil.
      9. Griffith Cooper and Sophia Favour.
May 2. William Hall and Livisy Slaughter.
      4. Charles Rouse and Nancy Butler.
     21. Lewis Rhodes and Fanny Orrell.
     25. Samuel Lecompte and Polly Price.
      " Noble Vickers and Rebecca Plummer.
June 2. Nathl. Perry and Sarah Harper.
      3. Christopher Swift and Francy Rolph.
        Solomon Robinson and Sophia C. Denny.
      9. Levi Dukes and Nancy Alcock.
        William McNeese and Lydia Hopkins.
     19. Thomas Mumfert and Elizabeth Lunarr.
     23. William Williams and Sarah Mason.
     26. Archibald Cohn and Triphenia Morgan.
      " William Faulkner and Prudence Towers.
     27. Charles Critchett and Ann Manship.
July 11. James Colescott and Polly Davis.
     16. Elijah Phillips and Betsy Dial.
      . James Dickinson and Letitia Price.
     21. John Saulsbury and Elizabeth Sharpe.
     23. Andrew Hall and Sarah Meeds.
August 1. Joshua Craynor and Naomi Vain.
     17. Daniel Voshell and Elizabeth Williams.
      " Jonathan Jacobs and Sarah Wright.
     19. Samuel Wooters and Sally Cartrope.
     20. William Connoly and Mary Jackson.
     25. John Cooper and Margaret Valliant.
      " Philemon Spencer and Eliza Boutle.
September 5. Thomas Boush and Eliza ———.

September 13. Nathaniel Ellsbury and Margarette Smith.
　　　　　16. Thomas Coursey and Mary Boon.
　　　　　　　Thomas Duhadaway and Mary Wright.
　　　　　20. William B. Smith and —— Downes.
　　　　　25. Cloudsbury Williamson and Polly Scott.
　　　　　29. Abner Roe and Mary Irwin.
　　　　　"　Christopher Driver and Polly Glann.
October　2. Nathan Cooper and Anna Stewart.
　　　　　7. Resdon Fountaine and Elizabeth ——.
　　　　　27. Thos. Brannock and Nancy Brannock.
　　　　　"　Shadriack Cooper and Rachel Shery.
November　3. Isaac Doram and Charlotte Henry.
　　　　　7. Thomas Hooper and Jane Burgess.
　　　　　16. Thomas Hicks and Eliza Alcock.
　　　　　17. John Boon and Peggy Mason.
December 10. James Clements and Mary Johnson.
　　　　　19. Henry Williams and Lydia Craynor.
　　　　　21. Joshua Cooper and Ann Wilson.
　　　　　27. William Priest and Betsy Dick.
　　　　　31. William Bourke and Elizabeth Gray.

1802.

January　4. Aaron Griffith and Nancy Colliston.
　　　　　5. James Caulk and Sarah Clough.
　　　　　　 Daniel W. Dickinson and Ann Richardson.
　　　　　12. William Roe and Patty Brades.
　　　　　17. John Sullivan and Rebecca Hubbart.
　　　　　19. Asbury Upaton and Nancy Hurd.
　　　　　21. Joseph W. Walls and Rebecca George.
　　　　　23. Vachel Keene and Sarah Fauntleroy.
　　　　　"　Shadrach Dean and Rebecca Ruse.
　　　　　"　Thomas King and Eliza. Lawrence.
　　　　　26. Peter Eaton and Rebecca Willis.
February　9. Robert Roe and Nancy Coxselle.
　　　　　16. Richard Whitby and Darkey Boon.
　　　　　20. John Wilson and Margaret Russell.
　　　　　"　Samuel Hardcastle and Francina Fall.
　　　　　24. Thomas Andrew and Amelia Dilton.

March 3. William Kelly and Elizabeth Willis.
" William Faulkner and Sally Gibson.
3. John Williams and Susannah Thomas.
9. John Gibson and Elizabeth Whitby.
14. John C. Lewis and Mary Ruver.
17. Robert Jarman and Elizabeth Genn.
30. John Camper and Polly Dean.
April 8. Aaron Dut and Anna Simpson.
21. William Downes and Mary Saulsbury, at Cambridge.
May 11. James Boon and Sarah Caramine.
25. Andrew Chilton and Catharine Davis.
28. Thomas Bright and Jane Robinson.
June 5. James Barwick and ―― ――.
15. Burton Faulkner and Elizabeth Barker.
July 6. Elisha Burt and Catharine Smootters.
" James Polwell and Sarah Bush.
" James Coursey and Rebecca Jackson.
10. John Ruth and Ann Seth.
14. Andrew Sullivane and Kitty Tims.
19. William Council and Polly Ewing.
20. John Satterfield and Ann Parkinson.
" William Brown and Margaret Longfellow.
28. Thomas Wherrett and Rebecca Covey.
August 16. John Barker and Celia Andrews.
17. Tilghman Andrew and Rebecca Currie.
18. Thomas Diggins and Wealthy Warner.
21. John Hunnsay and Charlotte ――.
25. William Warner and Polly Diggins.
27. William Boon and Rebecca Saulsbury.
" William Saulsbury and Tamsey Dodd.
28. James Plumer and Eliza Taylor.
" James Griffith and Mariaim Morris.
September 2. Tilghman Warner and Rhoda Stevens.
4. William Bonner and Charity Willis.
27. James Stranghan and Priscilla Slaughter.
October 19. S. Wootten and Levice Wright.

October 26. Peter Richardson and Nancy Mowbray.
November 5. Joel Clements and Margaret Roe.
" Richard Swift and Minty Baggs.
" Neal Rhodes and —— Higmitt.
18. Thos. Saulsbury and Nancy Downes.
December 1. Athel Stewart and Sarah Dudley.
" Henry Harris and Rebecca Downes.
20. Thomas Chambers and Elizabeth Priest.
21. Dennis Eaton and Mary Chilcutt.
22. Nathan Barwick and Mary Kinnerront.
23. Noah Slaughter and Esther Keon.
" Henry Banberry and Eliza Malcolm.
30. William Colscott and Eliza Miller.
31. James Clements and Anna Swift.

1803.

January 7. John Longfellow and Jane Walker.
7. William Stevens and Letta Gowtee.
17. James Byrn and Henrietta Meeds.
25. Henry Jones and Eliza Taylor.
February 1. William Dut and Ann Layton.
2. Washington Young and Ann ——.
8. Alex. Challslum and Rebecca Whitby.
11. Solomon Dean and Eliza Stevens.
March 3. Nathan Bradley and Winnifred Willis.
8. John Morriston and Lydia Frampton.
April 1. Rebecca Clements and Tamza Morris.
7. William Jump and Ann Price.
12. Samuel Booker and Leah Coper.
20. John Doe and Sarah Roe.
27. Ebraham Jump and Lidney Carter.
May 3. Samuel Emerson and Mary Butler.
11. William Steel and Maria Price.
17. Brownell Melvin and Margaret Craddock.
20. M—— Collison and Sarah Cade.
June 6. George Hall and Mary Steedham.
7. John Cahall and Margaret Shaw.

June 11. Samuel Garner and Mary Baker.

18. Alexander Talson and Sallie Councill.

21. William Kelley and Rachel Leverton.

July 5. Stephen Sheiron and Sidney Williamson.

26. Nass Roe and Lydia Whittington.

28. Jesse Founder and Margaret Eagle.

" William Cavin and Margaret Stevens.

August 13. Charles Morgan and Stirling Andrew.

24. Olive [?] Saulsbury and Charlotte Griffin.

31. Thomas Willis and Launtia Willis.

September 3. James M. Broom and Ann Driver.

15. Elisha Milford and Celia Willis.

20. Henry Swiggett and Henrietta Mitchell.

" John Boon and Priscilla Fountain.

October 6. Thomas Smith and Charlotte Blunts.

8. Nathan Russell and Elizabeth Sparks.

11. John Thomas and Mizza Lloyd.

11. Isaac Anderson and Mary Smith.

18. William Thowley and Sarah Sylvester.

29. Nathan Shawmhawn and Frances Nicols.

November 8. Charley Prin and Deborah Hunter.

9. John Martin and Nany Eaton.

11. James Baueker and Hiphena Thomas.

11. Edward Holbrook and Mabel Boon.

16. Stephen Stanford and Henrietta Clark.

" William Reese and Sarah Sharpe.

22. Richard Wilson and Sophia Satterfield.

26. Channy Ridgaway and Elizath Carty.

28. Edward Barwick and Sarah Hubbard.

29. William Oxenham and Fanny Price.

December 6. John Collscott and Sarah Stevens.

7. Curtis Connelly and Sarah Carmine.

13. Mordicaw —— and Elizth. Oram.

15. Stephen Rynor and Anna Casson.

20. —— Fountain and Sally May.

" William Towers and Margaret Wooters.

20. Thomas Turpin and Sarah Richardson.

December 21. William Smith and Sarah Dean.
      Thomas Hurd and Marry Harris.
    22. Thos. Carpenter and Deborah Kinnamon.
    24. Lodman Shields and Rachel George.
    28. Philip Russom and Nanny Knatts.
    30. Joseph Newham and Naomy Andrew.

1804.

January 5. James Newnoe and Christianna Brown.
    12. James Caulk and Rebecca Keene.
    26. Joseph Durdon and Susan Sangston.
    31. Abner Roe and Elizabeth Satterfield.
    " Levy Russom and Cynthia Knotts.
February 4. John Wootters and Fanny Willis.
    Daniel Swiggett and Elizabeth Mathews.
    6. Tristram Carman and Jenny Dawson.
    8. Daniel Bartlett and Trippinah Cohic.
    " William Jones and Jane Roe.
March 5. George Ringgold and Sarah Ratcliff.
    10. Edward Carter and Nanny Whitby.
    13. Henry Casson and Addah Swift.
    16. Isaac Pool and Lydia Wright.
    17. Thomas Chambers and Polly Faulkner.
    19. Stephen Wing and Esther Nash.
    27. John Clements and Rachel Newell.
    29. Henry Thawley and Sarah Hunter.
April 5. James Edmondson and Sophia C. Robinson.
    9. Robert Roun and Sarah Seword.
    10. Edward Thowley and Nancy Ringgold.
    17. Henry Mason and Nanny Johnson.
    21. John Dean and Margaret Kinnamont.
    25. Nathan Satterfield and Peggy Rudd.
May 29. James Gray and Charlotte Hudson.
June 5. Nathan Baynord and Sarah ——.
    13. James —— and Sarah Lee.
    18. Clement Todd and Darkas Fountain.
    23. John Williams and Rubecah Tamson.

June 25. Thomas McGuire and Channy Carman.
    26. Nathl Satterfield and Elizth. Cahalle.
    " James Morgan and Mary Andrew.
July 14. John Ross and Pheby Boon.
    24. John Smith and Rhoda Perry.
    " Thomas Beal and Hannah Swift.
    25. Jacob Hickman and Britania Eaton.
    30. James Wheatley and Elizth. Morton.
    31. John Pritchett and Rachel Spencer.
August 11. Wm. D. Glover and Sally Byor.
    18. James Harvey and Nanny Johnson.
    " Daniel Lyon and Fanny Camper.
    28. Henry Martindall and Nany Dwoaikbure.
September 1. John Kinnamon and Mary Webber.
    15. Thomas Connolly and Lydia Harvey.
    18. William Parratt and Anna Kirby.
    21. William Willoughby and Esther Hopkins.
    29. Joseph Dean and Nany Cop——.
October 3. Lawrence Porter and Margaret Morgan.
    " Joshua Williams and Margaret Thorp.
    23. Samuel Mason and Margaret Clarke.
    24. Beauchamp Eaton and Margaret Stubbs.
November 6. Anderson Porter and Jane Ewing.
    " Allen Wood and Fanny Warren.
    12. Andrew Lord and Margaret Collins.
    21. Samuel Black and Grace Darem.
    29. Thos. Richardson and Sarah Denny.
December 11. Andrew Fountain and Elizabeth Moore.
    18. Joseph Coxe and Priscilla Roe.
    " Joseph Wood and Rachel Plummer.
    31. Shadrick Chilcutt and Elizabeth Blades.
    " Thomas Ruse and Margaret Andrew.

1805.

January 1. Martain Alford and Britanna Pritchett.
    2. William Slaughter and Prudence Taylor.
    5. Emory Russell and Ann Morgan.

January 8. Selte Sprouce and Lucretia Turner.
February 1. William Jackson and Rebecca Faulkner.
      " Alexander Griffith and Mary Collison.
      5. Hugh Valliant and Helender Taylor.
   11. James M'Comb and Elizabeth Lindere.
   12. James Sharwood and Nanny Tailor.
   16. Emory Satterfield and Elizabeth Colgan.
   26. Fredk. Halbrook and Rachel Craynor.
March 1. John Stevens and Elizabeth Willis.
      8. William Coursey and Sarah Jones.
April 20. Henry Nicholson 3rd and Elizabeth Sellers.
May 7. Samuel Coursey and Rebina Kirby.
   25. Thomas Connor and Rhoda Eaton.
   25. William Higniett and Sarah Peters.
   30. Benjamin Kemp and Sally Price.
June 17. Thomas Thawley and Nancy King.
   22. John White and Levey Wingate.
   25. William Thawley and Nanny Jump.
July 9. Thomas Valliant Jr. and Anna Tarton.
   11. John Green and Mary Swan.
   21. Henry Meeds and Martha Ashford.
   23. James Thawley and Rebina Boon.
   27. Thomas Kemp and Ann Prouse.
   30. Levin Wingate and Margaret Meeds.
August 3. William Cannon and Milliy Emory.
      7. Richard Saulsbury and Rachel Smith.
   14. William Fountain and Ann Cooper.
   17. Benjamin Atwell and Rebina Soward.
   28. Francis Elliott and Sarah Wirthgolt.
   29. Elijah Russell Jr. and Ann Talboy.
September 3. David Roe and Nanny Wilson.
   11. Andrew Manship and Margaret Russell.
   23. Thomas Plummer and Margaret Holland.
   24. Joseph Carmine and Elizabeth Fitzpatrick.
   26. John Barns and Eleanor Warren.
October 14. Warner Busteed and Sarah Bell.
   17. Caleb Connelly and Polly Blades.

October 24. Reuben Vane and Rhoda Bitlitor.
November 30. Henry Austin and Rachel Young.
Robert Cade and Ann Austin.
Mathew Traverse and Sally Poh.
Andrew Collison and Nelly Stubbs.
Mathew Saulsbury and Elizabeth George:
December 9. James Ruh and Araminta Hard.
16. John Malony and Elizabeth Charles.
21. Solomon Carter and Sarah Puraelle.
25. John Jackson and Mary Ann Webber.
28. Samuel Denny and Rebecca Thawley.
31. Thomas Binding and Sophia Harvey.
" James Wheeler and Frances Willis.
" Simeon Johnson and Rebecca Rouse.

1806.

January 11. George Graham and Henrietta Willis.
15. Joseph Newman and Ann Willoughby.
20. John Delanaway and Mary Jones.
23. John Beauchamp and Mary Driver.
" Thomas Smith and Charlotte Martindall.
29. Peter Chilcutt and Elizabeth Smith.
February 4. Edward Price and Margaret Casson.
6. Thomas Cooper and Rebecca Bell.
11. William Andrew and Rebecca Harris.
13. William Harris and Lucretia Ward.
March 7. Moses Craynor and Nancy Seneca.
8. Thomas Sylvester and Margaret Stradley.
10. Charles Hubbard and Ruth Lawler.
13. William P. Rolph and Sarah Nawlee.
15. Acquilla Vinson and Nancy Vinson.
18. Jacob Carmean and Susan Orum.
19. John Dute and Rachel Simpson.
27. James Clements Jr. and Mary Roe.
April 3. William Poor and Nanny Barker.
4. Moses Hopkins and Sarah Plummer.
10. Thomas Jenkins and Mary Pigg.

April 19. Jeremiah Rhodes and Elizabeth Orrell.
  25. John Dean and Amelia Nicols.
  26. Shadrach Glanding and Alice Barwick.
  29. Williams Summers and Dolly Fab.
May 19. Robt. Hutchinson and Keziah Partridge.
  24. Ambrose Hobbs and Elizabeth Cannon.
  27. Stephen Lewis and Margaret Ruband.
June 7. Elijah Morris and Martha Morgan.
  10. David Smith and Celia Swiggett.
  21. Peter Eaton and Rachel Eaton.
July 19. Jesse Leverton and Mary Eaton.
  22. Abner Leah and Mary Chairs.
August 2. Garretson Blades and Ann Mitchell.
  9. Charles Mittle and Lydia Swann.
  19. Richard Price and Isabella Austin.
  20. Vinson Emerson and Mary Austin.
  26. Thomas Larimore and Mary Blades.
  27. Samuel Cradock and Nanny Baynord.
September 6. William Fisher and Keziah Boon. ¿
  9. Samuel Denny and Sarah Jones.
  16. Noah Eaton and Nancy Scadrick.
  " Edgell Scondrach and Ann Pirt.
  17. Mathew Hardcastle and Polly Willis.
  26. Andrew Bawning and Sally Bowdle.
  27. Sullivane Bell and Rachel Jump.
October 14. Walter Jenkins and Elenor Valliant.
  15. Richard Philips and Javenty Pratty.
  " Thomas Swann and Sarah Roe.
November 5. George Reed and Mary Harrington.
  7. Bruffett Vinson and Ann Roe.
  8. Henry Costen and Ann O'Bryan.
  15. William Jester and Nancy Coursey.
  " Daniel Bartlett and Elizabeth Harris.
  27. William Cahall and Elizabeth Cox.
  Nathan Jones and Sarah Swift.
December 2. John McCombs and Cynthia Ridgaway.
  11. Andrew Reed and Elenor Causey.

December 13. William Burtt and Mary Pippin.

" Noah Swift and Elizabeth Meredith.

16. Curtis Eaton and Lavica Connelly.

20. Benjamin McNeese and Mary Faulkner.

23. Ephraim Greenhawk and Lydia Taylor.

25. Daniel Anthony and Abigail Garey.

26. Jesse Blades and Elizabeth Thomas.

27. Nathaniel Thomas and Elizabeth Cavender.

31. William Cahall Jr. and Frances Roe.

1807.

January 8. Richard Hudson and Elizabeth Dillen.

10. Thomas Turner and Sally Sparklin.

13. William Gardner and Naney Young.

14. James Sweedlin and Sophia Porter.

27. Jonathan Eaton and Mary Stubbs.

29. Brumovell Millven and Margaret P. Wilson.

" William G. Smith and Nancy Dawson.

February 6. Zechariah Goutee and Mary Stevens.

14. Joseph Frampton and Peggy Carner.

17. Samuel Thawley and Elizabeth Elliott.

27. John Berry and Ann Kelly.

March 3. Thomas Seymore and Mary Ann Turner.

3. Henry Austin and Mary Warner.

4. Richard Keene and Henrietta Boon.

Richard Stubbs and Roda Hall.

21. Andrew Morgan and Mary Morrison.

25. Nathan Hobbs and Anna Dillen.

28. Henry Dean and Ann Blades.

" Jesse Wood and Elizth. Butler.

April 1. Charles Dean and Prudence Ruh.

2. John Harrington and Sarah Countess.

9. Thomas Jaikson and Mary Dawson.

11. John Jaikson and Rachel Russum.

25. Jacob Diel and Margaret Critchett.

" Samuel Crayner and Ann Pearce.

29. Bennett Wherrett and Peggy Saulsbury.

May   2. Isaac Swan and Nancy Chance.
   19. John Cox and Izabella Harrington.
June 2. Joseph Boon and Tilly Mason.
   11. James Keene and Eliza Ann Lucindy Carney.
   16. David Neal and Elizabeth Kelley.
July 1. Caleb Smith and Comfort Russell.
   8. Saulsbury Cannon and Ann Critchett.
   21. Thomas Wibber and Nancy Garrett.
   29. William Milson and Thisay Pippin.
   30. Curtis Beauchamp and Nancy Clarke.
   31. John Pennington and Eliza Mumford.
August 6. James Lane and Relena Slaughter.
   " Thomas Hill and Charlotte Smith.
   11. Daniel Young and Sarah Cheiznon.
   " Anaren Willoughby and Hersey Jenkins.
   12. Charles Hubbard and Rebena Anthony.
   14. Thomas Bradly and Rebena Baynord.
   15. Major Bradley and Sophia Caldwell.
   25. Curtis Dean and Keziah Williams.
   " John Plummer and Mary Turner.
   29. George Brownie and Sarah Pritchett.
   " Levin Eaton and Mary Cockrin.
September 1. Henry Bolton and Mary Holmer.
   " Solomon Dean and Lilly Dill.
   29. Samuel Mathews and Nancy Roe.
October 22. James Sangston and Sarah Stevens.
   23. Capy Pritchett and Lydia Willoughby.
November 7. James Greenlee and Esther Willoughby.
   10. Richard Mason and Sarah Scott.
   16. Zachariah Winwright and Nelley Davis.
   23. Timothy Caldwell and Nancy Williams.
   28. Thomas Sylvester and Rachel Hopkins.
December 8. Gilbert Scott and Ann Roe.
   14. Joshua Wright and Nancy Hutchinson.
   19. John Shanks and Lydia Baynard.
   30. Isaac Nicols and Elizabeth Fountain.

1808.

January 2. Eli Sharklin and Nancy Nicols.
5. John Williamson and Britannae Todd.
6. Thomas Orem and Rachel Brown.
12. Nathan Grayless and Sarah Evitt.
13. John P. Price and Mary Davis.
19. James S. Colscott and Lucretia Hardesty.
23. Michael Bateman and Sarah Merrick.
" John Saulsbury and Margaret Manship.
February 1. James Pearce and Ann Green.
9. William Sewell and Lucretia Cannon.
13. Gilden Hughcall and Mary Wilson.
22. Gilbert Faulkner and Elizabeth Dill.
25. William Chilton and Nancy Postlethwaite.
25. Jonathan Grault and Lydia Knotts.
March 7. Andrew Fountain and Nancy Fountain.
8. Thomas Hubbard and Mary Lyons.
" William Connolly and Sophia Eaton.
23. William Burton and Susan Wright.
27. Nathan Slaughter and Celey Bartlett.
April 2. Henry Grayham and Elizabeth Smith.
9. John Chilcutt and Ann Rouse.
9. Isaac Bayley and Mary Fountain.
Daniel Webster and Elizabeth Wilson.
19. Saml. Pinfield and Sarah Hye.
26. Josiah Ginn and Margaret Newcomb.
May 3. Peter Wilson and Ann Roe.
10. William Gardner and Rebecca Carpenter.
20. Jesse Eaton and Peggy Bartlett.
27. William Green and Rita Rigby.
29. Stephen Lucas and Sally Keene.
June 11. Daniel Smithe and Elizabeth Price.
14. Samuel Carter and Nancy Croney.
17. William Lowe and Rebecca Wolcott.
18. Lloyd Lord and Elizabeth Knotts.
July 12. Absalom Meredith and Margaret Hines.
30. Tilghman Todd and Mary Fountain.

5

August 6. Robert Jones and Elizabeth Willis.
   11. Benjamin Faulker and Nancy Clough.
   13. Ambrose Hobbs and Nancy Stevens.
   15. John Comica and Ann Baynard.
September 3. Edward Street and Sarah Barnes.
   6. Daniel Stevens and Nancy Cannon.
   " James Gray and Nancy Sherman.
   10. Joseph Kidd and Elizabeth Morris.
   20. James Bartlett and Mary Roe.
   29. John Saulsbury and Margaret Virden.
October 3. James Wright of John and Mary Kelley.
   10. Andrew Benchamp and Nancy Andrew.
   15. Staten Berry and Nancy Morriston.
   " Pierre W. Stewart and Sarah Carroll.
   " John Baynard and Rachel Harris.
   22. Aaron Duke and Rebecca Blades.
November 12. James Butler and Mary Smith.
   14. Levin Charles and Mary Hurd.
   16. Henry Covington and Ann Fisher.
December 8. John Pronce and Elizabeth Johnson.
   13. Henry Friend and Mary Aldridge.
   16. Casson Fountain and Martha Fisher.
   28. James Harrison and Nancy Martindale.
   30. Michael Hubbard and Rhoda Sullivan.
   31. Peter Pinfield and Mary Harris.

1809.

January 2. Levi Chance and Sally Roe.
   3. John Andrew and Tamsey Andrew.
   4. George Collison and Sally Lyden.
   7. John Graham and Anna Ritta Dawson.
   7. Thomas Kirby and Britanne Morgan.
   9. James Nooner and Lydia Morriston.
   12. James Allen and Elizabeth Powell.
   19. Solomon Clifte and Anne Clarke.
   24. John Handy and Rebecca Nicols.
   " Henry Pearce and —— Townsend.

January 25. Joseph Clarke and Mary Hudson.
February 1. John Riley and Nancy Hudson.
    Arthur Willis and Nancy Wright.
   9. Henry Willoughby and Philadelphia Willoughby.
  20. Levin Willoughby and Darcos Stuart.
  21. Nathan Shaunahan and Esther Brooks.
  27. Collison Pritchett and Nancy Peters.
  28. Austin Foster and Henny Stokes.
  28. Nathan Monticue and Elizabeth Boon.
March 14. William Whiteley and Elizabeth Baynord.
  14. James Johnson and Nancy Whiteley.
  14. Henry Austin and Elizabeth Austin.
  21. Parrott Roe and Rebecca Roe.
April 1. Azle Stevens and Nancy Andrew.
  4. William Fountain and Sarah Barton.
  17. Ezekiel Gullitt and Lucretia Jump.
  18. William Wheatley and Bath. Chance.
  24. Eli Connelly and Margaret Johnson.
May 4. Levin Stack and Sally Brown.
  8. Thomas Vinson and Margaret Stokes.
  19. John Burnett and Sally Neall.
  20. John Barrott and Polly Hurd.
  31. William Hooper and Sally Clark.
June 8. Levi Russom and Sally Bradley.
   " James Pearce and Elizabeth Colston.
  14. Richard Cantwell and Levisa Andrew.
  21. Samuel Lucas and Ann McCormick.
July 16. William Rich and Henrietta Glover.
  17. William Aarons and Rebecca Holland.
  18. Gibson Andrew and Rebecca Townsend.
  22. Christopher Smith and Polly Caulk.
  25. William Polk and Livinia Causey.
  29. William Wales and Elizabeth Dawson.
August 4. Charles Clayton and Hannah Chambers.
  8. Benjamin Hall and Betsey Binding.
  9. William Pratt and Mary Carmean.

August 17. Henry Jaqnes and Sarah Hopkins.
   19. Nathan Corkin and Rebecca Willis.
   22. Peter Hinsley and Rebecca Chambers.
   26. George Newlee and Hannah Burte.
   30. Washington Adams and Jane Wolford.
   "   Evans Price and Susan Burton.
September 4. James Manlove and Jane Turner.
   5. James Barwick and Anna Price.
   6. William Roe and Sally Pearce.
   13. George Bozman and Nancy Sharpe.
   25. Weedon Thawley and Mary Whittington.
October 4. David Anthony and Nancy Alls.
   6. Jesse Hubbard and Elizabeth Kelly.
   9. Abner Roe and Nancy Harris.
   10. Charles Jewell and Elth. Erwin.
   13. Samuel Parker and Elizabeth Nobll.
   31. Pennell Emerson and Hannah Turner.
November 2. Thomas Pearson and Ann Anthony.
   16. Thomas Willis and Lovey Cranor.
   23. Benson Dill and Polly Kinney.
December 2. Richard Swift and Sarah Brown.
   6. Garman Cade and Nancy Dulaney.
   19. Gove Smith and Rosannah Lewis.
   20. William Jewell and Sarah Jewell.
   23. Charles Gielding and Elizabeth Swift.

1810.

January 16. Andrew Sheppard and Nelly Pritchett.
   25. Edward Flinn and Nancy Saulsbury.
   30. Tilghman Connelly and Ann Satterfield.
February 8. Richard Gore and Ann Barwick.
   9. Isaac Robinson and Sarah Wing.
   12. William T. Clarke and Rachel Boon.
   14. Edward Gibson and Louisa Parkinson.
   17. John B. Smith and Polly Fountain.
   20. Jacob Derochbrane and Polly Welsh.
   21. Fountain Collison and Elizabeth Draper.

March 6. Solomon Kenton and Margaret Hambleton.
        16. Henry Fisher and Rebecca Kelly.
May 2. Levin Stevens and Polly Rich.
June 6. William Raynard and Polly Warren.
        12. Stephen Dawley and Nancy Everingham.
        23. Emanuel Swift and Elizabeth Jump.
        25. Thomas Kinsley and Eleoner Sylvester.
        30. Abraham Thompson and Margaret Plummer.
July 2. Henry Emory and Henrietta M. Blake.
        12. James Roe and Mary Mood.
      " Isaac Smith and Sally Laverton.
        27. Ezekiel Trice and Elizabeth Chilent.
August 4. Nathan Brown and Nelly Johnson.
      " Thomas Culbreth and Ann Hardcastle.
        16. Solomon Wooters and Elizabeth Ross.
        27. Jeremiah Beauchamp and Sally Chilcutt.
        29. John McDaniel and Mary Cornelius.
September 21. Thomas Genn and Nancy Bradley.
      " David Neale and Celia Collins.
October 13. Thamas Black and Elizabeth Brown.
        30. Jonas Farrowfield and Elizabeth Price.
November 14. Joseph Miller and Elizabeth Baynord.
        17. John Lane and Elizabeth Isgitt.
December 4. Nimrod Andrew and Nancy Collins.
        15. Daniel Cheezum and Sarah Walker.
      " Edward Todd and Elizabeth Sullevane.
        20. John Clements and Nancy Milburn.
        26. William Manship and Ann Plummer.
        28. John A. Batchelder and Lucy Harding.
        29. Peter Covey and Peggie Eaton.

1811.

January 2. David Harrington and Elizabeth Catrip.
        11. John Poor and Nancy Genn.
        15. Edward I. Wilson and Henrietta Brooke.
      " James Le Compte and Elizabeth Le Compte.
        23. Garretson Reese and Deborah Willoughby.

January 24. Jeremiah Vinson and Elizabeth Johnson.
    25. Samuel Andrew and Lesha Carroll.
    28. Isaac Ridout and Sarah Mattee.
    29. James Meloney and Mary Williams.
February 8. Charles Stokes and Ann Leach.
    18. Mathew Stokes and Elizabeth Jones.
    21. Anthony Ross and Elizabeth Richardson.
    28. Benjamin Roe and Angeline Briley.
March 12. James Wootter and Sarah Vincent.
    " John Fisher and Tamsey Peters.
    " Peter Jump and Rachel Austin.
    19. John Hynson and Sally Jones.
    19. Thomas Boyce and Sarah Johnson.
April 4. James Horney and Mary Keene.
    5. Daniel Caulk and Priscilla Roe.
    16. Richard Wilson and Ann Matilda Cole.
    20. Jeremiah Rhoads and Rachel Seth.
    25. Jeremiah Marriss and Sarah Clarke.
May 4. Levin Hicks and Elizabeth Loveday.
    14. Nicholas W. Dorsey and Elizabeth Strangton.
June 6. David Sylvester and Mary Clements.
    6. Robert Stevens and Hester Driver.
    18. William Turner and Ann Dudley.
July 8. Levin Wert and Sarah Dean.
    9. Andrew Clarke and Lydia Bartoe.
    19. William Adams and Julianna Blunt.
    23. Jesse Collins and Peggy Andrew.
    27. Nicholas Millington and Lucretia Blades.
August 14. Thomas Bending and Lotty Stokes.
    15. Thomas Duhadaway and Rebecca Faulkner.
    17. James Caulk and Mary Hayes.
    21. Elijah Blades and Polly Bowdle.
    22. Joseph Harrison and Peggy Emerson.
    27. Robert Fountain and Jane Clendening.
    28. Peter Chance and Ann Webber.
September 5. Abraham Trice and Sally W. Clayland.
    19. Joseph Anthony and Nancy Turner.

September 23. William Colston and Deborah Barwick.
   24. Nathan Grayless and Charlotte Johnson.
   26. William Faulkner and Delia Moore.
   26. Daniel Helms and Lehaner Haddox.
   26. John Lister and Mary Kidden.
October 5. Thomas Wood and Kezia Morgan.
   8. John Perry and Fanny Lucas.
   10. Charles Tildon and Sally Townsend.
   22. Sylvester Cannon and Kitty Davis.
   28. Levin Watkins and Milly Andrew.
   " Richard Andrew and Mary Story.
November 20. Jeremiah Jefferies and Amelia Wainwright.
   27. Jacob Gordon and Susan Kemp.
   29. John Sterling and Sophia Smith.
   30. John Newman and Patty Jewell.
December 7. William Orrell and Mary Hardcastle.
   17. Noah Chance and Polly Thawley of Edward.
   21. Ephraim Draper and Mary Cooper.
   27. Thomas Dunawin and Polly Anderson.
   31. William Nicols and Elizabeth Dawson.

1812.

January 2. John Wilson and Mary Moore.
   3. Garretson Turner and Sally Gowty.
   11. William Millington and Ann Knotts.
   18. Southy Prewett and Rachel Kelly.
   24. Thomas Vandyke and Sally Hooper.
February 1. Mathew Harding and Polly Wheatley.
   5. Elijah Chance and Rebecca Vaulk.
   23. Giles Haky and Henrietta Fountain.
   26. Peter Morgan and Rachel Cockein.
March 4. Thomas Walker and Rebecca Cox.
   9. Daniel Brown and Lavinia Stevens.
   10. Abel Griffith and Mary Stevens.
   26. John Collison and Elizabeth Butler.
   31. John Seth and Nancy McGinnis.
April 11. George Prouse and Ann Satterfield.

April 15. Daniel Anthony and Sally Faulkner.
 22. James Sangston and Ann Robinson.
 24. Solomon Pippin and Fanny Brown.
May 5. William Waddell and Nancy Davis.
 " Nehemiah Allen and Henry Jewell.
 " Samuel Chance and Ann Pinfield.
 7. William Alford and Ann Crawford.
 18. George Andrew and Elizabeth Morgan.
 21. William Sewell and Lovey Carmine.
July 2. Robert Porter and Ann Cradock.
 21. Henry Jump and Marice Parrott.
 25. John Irvine and Elizabeth Hughes.
 28. Andrew Baggs and Fanny Strangton.
 " Mier Cahill and Elizabeth Briley.
 30. Robert Sylvester and Mary Duhaniel.
August 4. Richard Harrington and Elizabeth Faulkner.
 6. Jesse Connelly and Sophia Thomas.
 20. Samuel Mackey and Mary Crawford.
 28. Samuel Satterfield and Sarah Willis.
September 5. Henry Willis and Sarah Porter.
 12. William Faulkner and Peggy Melville.
 17. Warren Dawson and Nancy Griffith.
 25. Emory Willis and Margt. Fornerder.
 26. Andrew Price and Rebecca Clarke.
 29. Richard Willoughby and Deborah Lawrence.
October 7. Elisha Draper and Ann Collison.
 15. Abraham Pritchett and Rodoh Kelley.
 20. Nathan Todd and Polly Fountain.
November 13. William Oldfield and Rebecca Cahall.
 14. George Spurry and Adolpha Stokes.
 " Richard Willoughby and Tamsey Gray.
 18. James Ridgeway and Nancy Jump.
 19. Brannock Smith and Peggy Esbary.
 25. Short Willis and Polly Griffith.
December 15. Risdon Smith and Mary Robinson.
 " John Morgan and Lucretia Whemett.
 16. William Kelley and Rachel Ward.

December 16. William Grayley and Elizabeth Hughey.
     26. Jonathan Butler and Ann Bush.
     29. Foster Boon and Rebecca Countiss.
     29. John Dupee and Nancy Lane.

1813.

January 2. Clement Hubbard and Sally Eaton.
     7. James Orrell and Elizabeth Orrell.
    11. Nathan Jump and Elizabeth Sylvester.
    12. Edward Pritchett and Nancy Wheeler.
    13. Solomon Twiford and Catharine Boon.
    14. Samuel Gelin and Fanny Barcus.
    16. Nathaniel Talbot and Rachel Hall.
    27. William Stubbs and Elizabeth Conaway.
February 3. David Harrington and Sarah Faulkner.
     6. Samuel Paine and Elizabeth Brown.
    13. Seth Russom and Mary Phillips.
    15. Elijah Fisher and Ann Scott.
    18. James H. Flcharty and Nancy Saunders.
    22. James Hubbard and Ann Cortin.
March 2. David Roe and Elizabeth Pippin.
     " Samuel Milbourn and Sarah Pippin.
     " James Banning and Polly Brown.
    18. William Wright and Rebecca Dukes.
    20. John Eaton and Rebecca Hicks.
    30. John Godwin and Elizabeth Hall.
     " Francis H. Hally and Elizabeth Taylor.
April 3. Henry Thawley and Sarah Chippey.
     3. Emanuel Cranor and Polly Wodman.
     5. Watson Fountain and Elizabeth Barwick.
     5. William Green and Mary McCarty.
     6. Joseph Bell and Fanny Le Compte.
     8. George Millington and Ann Scott.
    20. William Keene and Allenora Pratt.
    29. Athel Stewart and Margaret Dudley.
June 1. Atwell Chance and Susan Baynord.

June 5. Robert Wootters and Mary Warner.
     15. Jesse Blades and Nancy Walker.
     23. Charley Grayless and Margaret Lucas.
July 17. John Lane and Elizabeth Cotner.
     20. Thomas Clendening and Letitia West.
August 25. Lewis Willis and Elenor Dillon.
      " George Newlee and Mary Burt.
September 4. Richardson Stubbs and Esther Watkins.
      8. Nathan Jones and Rebecca Rich.
      9. William Haghlett and Many Richards.
      " James Pearce and Mary Roberts.
     15. James Perry and Charity Carlile.
     17. Levin Murphy and Hannah Taylor.
     22. Thomas Wainwright and Rebecca Bordey.
     23. William Morgan and Elizabeth Taylor.
     27. Thomas Corkin and Elizabeth Snow.
October 7. Jonathan Porter and Nancy Russom.
      9. George Dill and Nancy Barney.
     12. John Emory and Caroline ——
     28. William Wootters and Levice Mathers.
      " Richard Skinner and Sophia Sudler.
November 2. Samuel Talbott and Anne Manship.
      " Purnell Fisher and Mary Wheeler.
      3. William Mittle and Peggy Andrew.
      9. —— Fountain and Sally Hall.
      " John Gainer and Henrietta Ross.
     25. Philip Le Compte and Peggy Willoughby.
December 14. John Stevens and Nancy Andrew.
     14. Richard Andrew and Sally Turner.
     16. George Manship and Mary Steel.
     18. John Clark and Elizabeth Barcus.
     21. Andrew K. Russell and Catharine Whiteley.
     22. Thomas Anderson and Elizabeth Dawson.
     23. John Gill and Elizabeth Shaw.
     24. Abel Gouty and Elizabeth Wheelton.
     29. John Hutson and Elizabeth Wilk.
     31. John Handcock and Susan Green.

1814.

January 6. William Oxenham and Hester Jump.
         12. Curtis Towers and Elizabeth Russell.
         18. Samuel Roe and Elizabeth Leath.
         22. Joseph Harrison and Mary Melony.
         24. Ezekiel Cooper and Louisa Baggs.
         31. Horatio Sharpe and Sarah Carroll.
February 1. Elijah Higinett and Sally Vincent.
         8. John Taylor and Elizabeth Jones.
      " Richard Gore and Fanny Wood.
        14. John Clarke and Ruth Vinson.
        15. Thomas Priest and Elizabeth Bradly.
March   3. Alex. C. Flynn and Sarah Holmes.
        15. Seth Godwin and Ann Harrington.
        22. Peter Todd and Rebecca Dean.
April   16. John Barces and Fanny Pratt.
      " John Simpson and Wilheminah Griffin.
May —. Noah Black and Margaret Keets.
        21. George Dawson and Rebecca Haddon.
        24. Bowdle Blades and Rhoby Tunely.
        31. Samuel Faulkner and Elizabeth McNeth.
      " Caleb Dehortz and Ann Price.
June   7. Thomas Postlethwait and Henrietta P. Hard-
          castle.
        18. James Carty and Sally Walker.
        23. Abraham Griffith and Mary Manship.
        27. James Seavy and Caroline Mathews.
        29. Greenbury Sullivan and Elizabeth Garey.
July 22. Nathaniel Thomas and Mary Baynord.
        25. Thomas Fountain and Mariah Coursey.
August 6. Noble Andrew and Ann Willes.
        8. James Hughes and Margaret Satterfield.
        8. John Fleharty and Fanny Harris.
        10. John Parkinson and Lydia Clarke.
        15. William Stewart and Mary Steel.
September 3. William Wheatley and Frances Newman.
        13. Thomas Breeding and Elizabeth Dukes.

September 14. Peter Chance and Elizabeth Greenhock.
      16. John Hutchings and Lydia Hughes.
October 19. Richard Flowers and Celia Blades.
      24. William Stevens and Ebey Andrews.
      26. George Prewitt and Mary Hordikin.
November 15. Joseph Crumpton and Ann Dillon.
      " Isaac Clements and Nancy Burtt.
December 1. Gideon Cooper and Mary Greenell.
      5. Thomas Council and Susan Williams.
      8. John Prouse and Sally Lord.
      10. Daniel Fountain and Margt. Quality.
      " Cretchu Lord and Lydia Harrington.
      17. Elijah Lyons and Sally Sullivan.
      " Levin Blades and Margaret Willis.
      20. Richard Lemar and Mary Williams.
      22. John Warner and Dorcas Carmean.
      24. Edward White and Elizabeth Hubbard.
      27. William Choffinch and Dorcus Manship.
      31. Thomas Williams and Elizabeth Chipman.
      " Allen Connelly and Margaret Davis.
      " William Covey and Ameleka Covey.

1815.

January 3. Absalom Adams and Mary Bartlitt.
      " Henry Carmean and Maria Walcott.
      4. Joseph Price and Sally Russom.
      5. Thomas M'Crakin and Fanny Strahan.
      9. Baynard Harris and Sarah Baily.
      11. John Hubbard and Ann Kelly.
      12. Vinson Morris and Sarah Stewart.
      16. Andrew Barton and Deliza Kelly.
      18. John Cheezum and Mary North.
      21. Samuel Lucas and Maria B. Manship.
      24. William Hurd and Elizabeth Rich.
February 2. Elijah Blades and Mary Dodd.
      2. Henry Collins and Mary Cranor.
      " Daniel Helm and Dorcas Lyons.

February 18. Aaron Wilson and Sarah Gill.

March 9. David M. Man and Lucy Choflinch.

11. Robert Bishop and Elizabeth Millington.

26. Solomon Brown and Henrietta Smith.

29. William Parrott and Eliza Chance.

April 26. Charles Price and Margaret Forman.

May 8. Aaron Lister and Nancy Warren.

10. Stephen Sanford and Rachel Sheppord.

25. Peter Holding and Mary Pearse.

June 1. Thomas Wadman and Margaret Saulsbury.

5. James Townsend and Deborah Connelly.

6. William Wright of Caleb and Elonor Dukes.

8. Merchant Cooper and Margaret Plummer.

13. Perry Pippin and Mary Newlee.

17. James Collins and Mary Adams.

" Isaac Hyatt and Ann W. Dickinson.

19. James Pearce and Harriet Charles.

27. Ennalls Collins and Mahala Harding.

29. Samuel Thayrp and Viney Wright.

July 4. Nathan Grayless and Sarah Le Compte.

6. Henry Meeds and Ann Blunt.

8. William Collins and Mary Wilkinson.

15. Isaac Cox and Sarah ——.

17. James Coalston and Frances E. Hardcastle.

20. William Miller and Rachel Coursey.

August 9. James Gray and Mehaley Hubbord.

14. William Keetes and Sarah King.

15. Samuel Trewitt and Ann Money.

20. Joseph P. W. Richardson and Lucy B. Potter.

23. Abner Roe and Elizabeth Miller.

" William Christopher and Mary Eaton.

31. John Harris and Sarah Stack.

September 1. Joshua Boon and Rebecco Bradley.

5. Thomas Burchenal and Juliana Errickson.

12. William Gibson and Isabella Watkins.

13. Henry Willoughby and Elizabeth Casson.

September 22. Edmond H. Owens and Margretta Turner.
    26. James Faulkner and Ann Collins.
    28. Nimrod Barwick and Nancy Webb.
October 6. Thomas Connelly and Sarah Davis.
    7. Elijah Fisher and Nelly Brown.
   24. Charles Willis and Nancy Steel.
November 16. William T. Coursey and Priscilla Sharp.
    20. Henry B. Hooper and Maria Jefferies.
    29. William Jewell and Susan Erwin.
December 9. John Roe and Ann Barwick.
   12. John Beauchamp and Mary Andrew.
   " Thomas Camper and Levica Rowens.
   " John Miller and Mary Kidd.
   14. Brison Gill and Ann Fountain.